Bookplates of the Kings

This edition is dedicated to
Guillermo de los Reyes,
with a nod to his regal name.

Bookplates of the Kings

Christine Price's
Catalogue of Royal Bookplates

Introduced and edited by Paul Rich

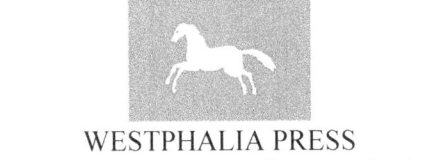

WESTPHALIA PRESS
An imprint of Policy Studies Organization

Bookplates of the Kings
Christine Price's
Catalogue of Royal Bookplates

Westphalia Press
An imprint of Policy Studies Organization
dgutierrezs@ipsonet.org

For information:
Westphalia Press
1527 New Hampshire Ave., N.W.
Washington, D.C. 20036

ISBN-13: 978-0-944285-82-4
ISBN-10: 0944285821

Updated material and comments on this edition can be found
at the Policy Studies Organization website:
http://www.ipsonet.org

Bookplates of the Kings:
Introduction to New Edition

LOUISE E. Winterburn (1864-1939) made a valuable gift
of bookplates to the San Francisco College for Women,
which then became part of the Library of the University of
San Francisco when the women's college joined forces with
the university. One of the founders of the San Francisco
Opera Association, she was both a collector and donor: in
1928 she is recorded as a supporter of the Department of
Prints at the Metropolitan Museum in New York.

It is by her bookplate collecting that she is known, and
especially for her specialization in royal plates. There are
collectors who are generalists in which they exchange and
purchase, but many realize that will not in the end
produce something of permanent value, and they pick a
field. The American Society of Bookplate Collectors and
Designers has been around since 1922 and facilitates
exchanges, and Ms. Winterburn was the president of a
like group, the California Bookplate Society.

The scope of the hobby can be appreciated by how the
British Museum could publish in 1900 a catalog of 35,000
plates in its Sir Augustus Franks Collection, and the
Dwen Pace collection of bookplates at Yale has more than
a quarter million examples. Obviously specializing as
exemplified in the Winterburn gift makes a lot of sense.
There are many categories from which to choose. Yale for
example has numerous donations of bookplates, including
those of Oxford and Cambridge libraries, of religious
orders, of the British West Indies, and of Finland. Some
famous artists have produced bookplates, including

Albrecht Durer, Marc Chagall, Rockwell Kent, and Paul Revere. The owners who had special plates made are equally celebrated and include George Washington, Queen Victoria, Sigmund Freud, Walt Disney, and J.P. Morgan. The choices are virtually innumerable.

So Ms. Winterburn was wise to pursue a theme. Many of the dynasties whose bookplates she acquired are no more, the casualties of war and political upheaval, but they live here in their bookplates.

Paul Rich

Catalogue of Royal Bookplates

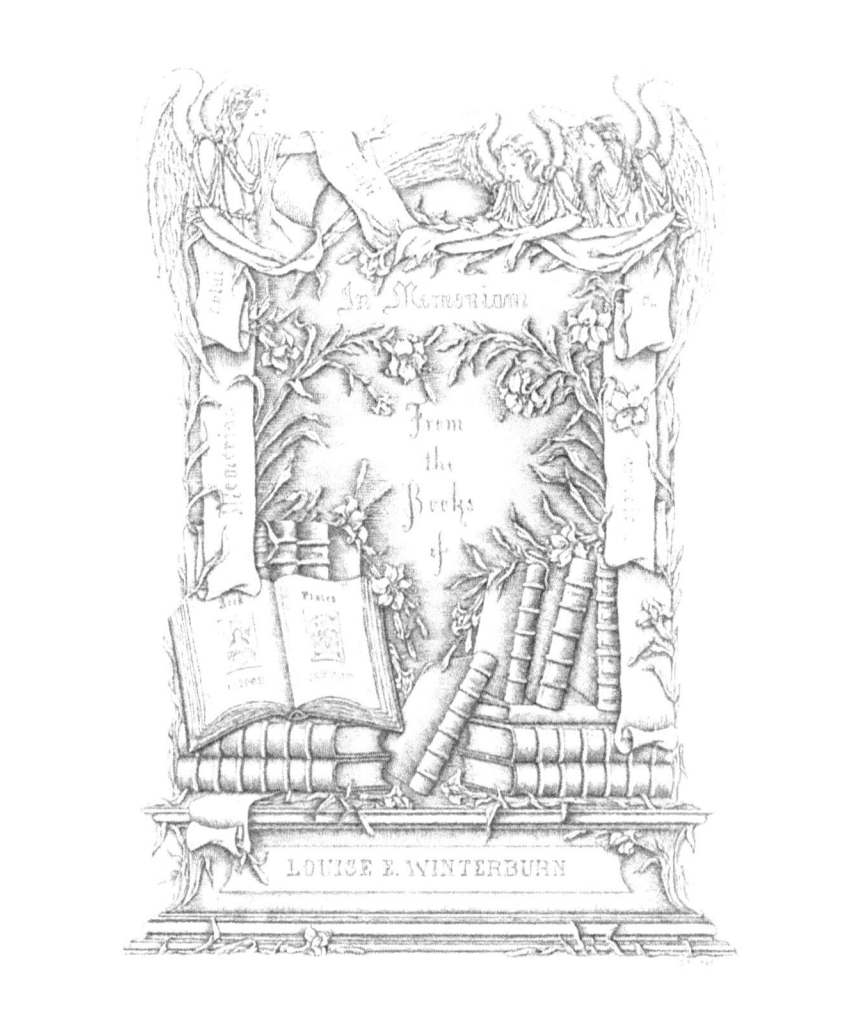

In Memoriam

From
the
Books
of

LOUISE E. WINTERBURN

Catalogue of

ROYAL BOOKPLATES

from the Louise E. Winterburn Collection
San Francisco College for Women

BY CHRISTINE PRICE

Frontispiece by Dorothy Payne

PRINTED FOR THE CALIFORNIA BOOKPLATE SOCIETY
BY THE SAUNDERS PRESS, CLAREMONT, CALIFORNIA
1944

THIS book is published by the members of the California Bookplate Society as a loving tribute to their late president

LOUISE E. WINTERBURN

Due to her unflagging energy, Miss Winterburn, in twelve short years, assembled an outstanding collection. Her many bookplates of Royalty and Nobility and of the eminent men and women of her generation, were acquired while countries and crowns were being overthrown and destroyed. Despite this upheaval, these treasures multiplied through the good will of many royal and noble potentates.

When Miss Winterburn recognized the educational and historical value of the collection, she decided to bequeath it as a token of love and affection to the Society of the Sacred Heart in her native city.

The collection now rests in the Rare Book Room of the Library of the San Francisco College for Women, located on the crest of San Francisco's historic landmark, Lone Mountain. For the courtesy of unrestricted access to the collection during the compilation of this work, the California Bookplate Society expresses grateful thanks to Reverend Mother Rosalie Hill R.S.C.J., Superior Vicar and Honorary president of the College.

VIOLA S. MEYER, *President,*
California Bookplate Society

September 23, 1942
San Francisco, California

Frontispiece

THE design for a bookplate for Louise Winterburn was conceived by Dorothy Payne in 1936. Miss Winterburn desiring that it be executed by one of the famous English engravers had begun correspondence with Alfred J. Downey, when death intervened. It therefore seems fitting that the bookplate should now take the form of a memorial.

Contents

Plates

(Catalogue number precedes the title of the bookplate)

Louise Eugenie Winterburn

An Appreciation

PATIENCE is the first virtue demanded of a bookplate collector, and without it and the discrimination to reject the lesser good for the greater, the Winterburn Collection would not have been possible.

The acquiring of ex libris designed for Royalty is one of the most difficult tasks a collector can undertake, requiring both courage and tact. The difficulties are manifold, for some royal households forbid the acquisition by a collector of the labels that mark their books.

Most of Miss Winterburn's collection came to her direct from the owner or the designer. Dealers sent their lists, and from these she selected with caution and intelligence. One plate was not accepted as authentic for three years. Two years went by before another beautiful bookplate, unattainable by the ordinary collector, was acquired.

As the collection grew, plates became more difficult to find. Months passed without the acquisition of an important item and the interim was spent in collecting a fund of information about the kings and queens whose bookplates were in the collection.

Miss Winterburn was never so happy as when she was sharing her joy in her latest acquisition or telling some humorous or charming story connected with her bookplates. Her generosity to other collectors was notable, her delight in fine workmanship very real.

As history-in-the-making has sent a number of kings and queens into exile, their ex libris—mementoes of their happier and more intimate lives—are precious.

MARGARET ELY WEBB

3

Biographical Sketch

To assemble the vital facts about the life of such a person as Louise Eugenie Winterburn, should be the task of an artist, or a poet. Louise Winterburn's shining, quiet life touched so many facets of western living, that no brief sketch can encompass them all.

She was born in San Francisco on the seventeenth of January, 1864, the fourth child of Joesph and Susanna (McDermott) Winterburn. Her birthplace was on Howard Street, then a fashionable district of the rapidly expanding city. Her mother, born in Philadelphia in 1839, came with her parents, in 1849, across the famous Overland Trail to Sacramento, living in California until her death in 1916. Her father was born in Northhampton, England, in 1834, and came with his family to California by way of Australia, in 1850. He became a printer and publisher and was one of San Francisco's leading business men for over fifty years.

San Francisco's civilization sprang into being without preliminary struggles and this early California metropolis provided a unique background for Louise Winterburn's formative years. Surplus wealth is the moving power that enables pioneer settlements to advance rapidly along social and intellectual lines, and wealth flowed into San Francisco from the beginning. The city had to its credit, twenty-four public and private schools within eight years from the discovery of gold. Both opera and the theatre flourished. The famous literary figures of the world came to see, and to tell of what they saw in the new El Dorado. Journalism also flourished, and a fertile production was reached more quickly than paper on which to print could be supplied.

Fashions and the "mode of the moment" were the latest

from Paris and the women were as well dressed as in any of the great style centers of the world. Few other American cities could offer growing young people a more cosmopolitan background. So Louise, a child of pioneer parents, grew up in these colorful early days. With her sister Minnie, and her three brothers, George, Charles and Edwin, the young Louise took part in the brilliant social life of the city; a social life more polished and urbane than the world has seen, before or since, in any inchoate community.

Louise's receptive mind absorbed much of the tradition which characterized early California life. Because of her father's close contact with the literary life of the city, she met many of the leaders who influenced the thought of the new western empire. Among the family friends were Mark Twain, Henry George, and William Keith.

Louise Winterburn's talents covered a wide range of activities: besides being an accomplished musician, she excelled in needlework in a period when it was developed to a fine art. With an acute sense of civic duty, her clear thinking mind played an important part in every civic matter with which she was concerned.

She had a warm sympathy with the problems of those closely associated with her, and a rare understanding of modern life. Her intimate contact with young people explains this in part for her nieces and nephews were very dear to her and she took a deep interest in their lives and the lives of their children.

Miss Winterburn's interest in bookplates was aroused through her friendship with Miss Adalène Brewer, whose brother, the Reverend William Augustus Brewer, had acquired a collection which was nationally famous. Dr. Brewer was the son of the Reverend Alfred Lee Brewer and with his father, was among the West's great educators.

In 1926, Miss Winterburn became a member of the California Bookplate Society, of which Dr. Brewer was one of the founders. In 1928, she was elected president of the Society and served in this capacity until her death.

It was in 1927, that she decided to specialize in Bookplates of Royalty, and in this she spared neither time nor expense. Hers was an untiring quest. She succeeded where others failed; and in a few short years had acquired a remarkable collection that has been viewed by collectors from many parts of the world. Through this pursuit, Miss Winterburn formed many interesting friendships and her correspondence gives a vivid record of her extensive activities in this chosen field.

Driven by a feeling that her work must be completed before the changing conditions in the world made the acquiring of such a collection impossible, she worked indefatigably. At intervals, during her last illness she was still indexing and filing the contents of the volumes. Shortly before her death, Miss Winterburn requested that the collection be taken to the College and placed where she had vizualized it for so many years.

Louise Winterburn's keen sense of humor, her patience and perseverance, and the spiritual beauty of her nature were an inspiration to all who came in contact with her. The world to her was not a strange and unfamiliar place but a wonderland of beautiful experiences; peopled with friends who exchanged their treasures for the riches yielded by her own distinctive personality. Small wonder that she left behind a memory of graciousness and charm! Small wonder that she left this world a better place than she found it!

Vale!

WHEATON BREWER

Recollection

Memorias colui mihi et amicis. This is the inscription that was prophetically chosen for the bookplate of Louise E. Winterburn. These words, so rich in meaning, recall a living memory of one endowed with quiet strength and gentle dignity—an example of gracious living in this modern world of confused values and false ideals.

The room where Miss Winterburn reviewed her collection for me was filled with hospitality and warmth. The soft blue at the windows, the work-box inlaid with mother-of-pearl, the jade and silver of miniture treasures—all exquisite implements of the gentle-woman, bespoke a long association with, and habituation to beauty.

A lamp shed its soft light upon an open scrap book, and across the table on which it lay, one faced the charming cicerone. For an instant one seemed to catch a glint of steel, the flash of a sword, or the gleam of a silken brocade worn by a tiara-crowned lady; for it was through castles, and towers, and history itself, that one was led, as the pages quietly succeeded one another. For perfection, one needed no further search; and the discrimination shown in the assembling of this collection revealed the true connoisseur.

Besides numerous other categories, the Winterburn collection contains the bookplates of Royalty from over twenty countries. Undoubtedly such a representative group could not have been amassed at any other period in the history of the world. With the present shifting of world events, one is certain that Louise Winterburn fulfilled a unique mission; as if by a fore-ordained coincidence, the decline of inherited rank occurred as her own life drew to its close.

Hers were the qualities exemplified in the truly royal, and

her bookplate collection represented an order which she herself unconsciously personified.

The passing of this gracious patrician is symbolic, marking as it does, the sunset of an era. From the tapestry of life that she has woven, there emerges a pagaentry, the splendor of which Louise E. Winterburn has immortalized through this miniature form of art, the ex libris. *Es memorias coluit sibi et amicis suis.*

Clare Ryan Talbot

Catalogue of Royal Bookplates

Introduction

To those who have had some acquaintance with the Louise E. Winterburn Collection of Bookplates in the San Francisco College for Women, it is apparent that this *Catalogue of the Royal Bookplates* covers only a small, though impressive, section of the whole. The entire collection of bookplates, placed within mounts, so as to be removable for exhibit, occupies forty-five leather-backed albums, with some separately mounted plates and hundreds of unmounted items. In addition, there are accompanying files of correspondence and about forty volumes of bookplate literature. A glance at the gold-stamped titles of the albums reveals the scope and importance of the collection: Royalty, Royal Institutions, Nobility, Clergy, Stage and Screen, Authors; and for artistic quality, all the accepted great in bookplate design: Barrett, Downey, Eve, Sherborn, Sidney L. Smith, Edwin Davis French, Arthur N. Macdonald, E. B. Bird, California's Margaret Ely Webb, and many others. There are separate groups of Norwegian and Czechoslovakian plates.

That the royal bookplates exist in sufficient number to be entitled a "collection" in their own right, constitutes an achievement on Miss Winterburn's part which is remarkable, and probably unique in the United States. It seems as if Miss Winterburn had seized that moment between wars, when bookplates could still be obtained from the homes of royalty in response to a gracefully worded appeal, or on the other hand, could be purchased from dealers, who, because of world stress, were more than usually well supplied with items that in more normal times would not have been available. The Russian plates are an example of this latter condition; for how otherwise than through the sale and dispersal of the imperial libraries, could these plates have become procurable? Many factors have now combined to drive the former ruling houses of Europe from power. National arms have been abrogated or simplified, revolution has replaced monarchy with the rule of the proletariat, and intermarriage of royalty and commoners has increased. Royal bookplates, except for England, are in a fair way to become museum pieces. And, because the collection is unusual, the catalogue itself assumes somewhat the nature of an original undertaking in the realm of bookplate literature. While some excellent publications are available for countries and periods, those dealing with the European royal scene as an entirety are apparently non-existent.

The catalogue follows the order in the "Royalty" albums of the Collection, and is in general by nationality. This has not proven an ideal arrangement as there are disturbing irregularities in country and chronology, which we trust will, however, be compensated for, in part at least, by the entries under geographical headings, as well as by persons, in the index. Album no. 1 is comprised in numbers 1 to 57; Album no. 2, numbers 58 to 103; Album no. 3, numbers 104 to 157; Album no. 4, numbers 158 to 181. The first 103 numbers are English, the remainder continental royalty. It is recognized that by strict definition all items are not "royal," but the association is almost invariably close, and none has been deleted. There are, in fact, additional plates which I regret have not been included in this category, notably for the Earl of Harewood and the Houses of Parliament.

Heraldic achievements have been presented descriptively, and not "technically." A rather less detailed delineation has been accorded the British coats of arms than the section which follows. It seemed that space might be conserved, and the users of the catalogue spared repetition and possible confusion, if a tabulation of the quarterings on the British shield were provided, to which general resort might be made for any given bookplate displaying arms. By "royal arms" is invariably meant the coat of arms borne by the sovereign at that particular date, and to which likewise any member of the Royal family would be entitled, when "differenced" with the appropriate coronet and "label." The table follows.

1603-1689. (1603, Scotland was added at the accession of James I) Quarterly 1 and 4 France modern (three fleurs-de-lis) and England (three "leopards" i.e. lions "passant," or in a leopard posture, counter-quartered) 2 Scotland (a lion "rampant"), 3 Ireland (a harp). Cf. no. 97, Charles II. Plate VIII.

1689-1702. (1689, accession of William and Mary) The lion of Nassau was added in pretence, and changes were made in arrangement to display the joint sovereignty. No example.

1702-1707. Queen Anne returned to the example of the Stuarts above. Cf. no. 100, William, Duke of Gloucester. Not illustrated.

1707-1714. (1707, union with Scotland) A new pattern was formed, quarterly 1 and 4 England impaled with Scotland, 2 France, 3 Ireland. No example.

1714-1801. (1714, Hanover added at the accession of George I) 1 England impaled with Scotland, 2 France, 3 Ireland, 4 Hanover, showing Brunswick (two "leopards"), Luneburg (a lion "rampant"), Westphalia (a horse "courant"), with an inescutcheon (the crown of Charlemagne) Cf. no. 60, George III. Plate XII.

1801-1837. (1801, arms of France removed) Quarterly 1 and 4 England, 2 Scotland, 3 Ireland, and Hanover moved to an escutcheon of pretence. Cf. no. 66, George IV. Plate XII.

1837-present day. (1837, accession of Queen Victoria, when Hanover removed) Quarterly 1 and 4 England, 2 Scotland, 3 Ireland. Cf. no. 11, Queen Victoria, Plate I; no. 22 George V (*While Prince of Wales*) Plate VI also shows Saxony on an inescutcheon of pretence, from the arms of the Prince Consort, as borne by his children and grandchildren, but dropped on ascent to the throne. With the change in the family name from Guelph to Windsor (1917), Saxony was deleted from all shields.

For our purposes then, briefly, with the omission of "tinctures," or colors, the insignia of a full royal achievement comprises, in addition to the quarterings on the shield, the crest (on a crown, a lion, crowned); the supporters (lion and unicorn, with the proper accoutrements); and the motto, "Dieu et mon droit," to which the sovereign alone is entitled. As the above motto is the invariable accompaniment of the arms of the British ruler, its presence is never specifically noted. For the same reason, "Honi soit qui mal y pense," motto of the "Most Noble Order of the Garter" (founded 1348) inscribed upon the garter, and thus forming an intrinsic part of it, is not restated each time, though inevitably present. Other insignia of the "Garter" include the collar, and the badge of the "George," sometimes called the "Great George," suspended from it, which portrays the patron saint mounted on a horse and slaying the dragon with a lance. The ruling sovereign is always head of the Order by virtue of birth.

In English royal heraldry the "label" is used to signify cadency. It consists of a bar, or ribbon, with three or more points, or pendants, and is issued by royal warrant, with the proper charges indicated (the Prince of Wales's label remains always three points, and is uncharged). Other marks of "difference" or cadency include the "baton" ("sinister" for illegitimacy), the "baton peri" used in France to indicate a younger son, or younger branch of the house, and the "bordure."

The royal arms of France, usually called "France modern" in contradiction to the early arms, "semée-de-lis" known as "France ancient," are three fleurs-de-lis. The arms of the Empire were a "French imperial eagle" grasping a sheaf of thunderbolts.

It remains only to explain a few heraldic terms, which have been used throughout the text and for which there exist no popular equivalents: *accollé,* placed side by side, in referring to two shields; *badge,* a device distinct from shield or crest, not a charge; *impaled,* two coats of arms placed side by side on the same shield; *lozenge,* a diamond-shaped figure, used in general to display a woman's arms, but many variations occur in practice. *Cipher* has been used interchangeably for a monogram or single initial; *ensigned* (adorned) has been used interchangeably for surmounted, in respect to a coronet or crown. It is to be recalled that the *dexter* (right) and *sinister* (left) sides of the shield are to be considered in inverse terms, or, from the point of view of the holder of the shield behind it, and not as it faces the observer.

In general, names, with accompanying titles of honor and address, have been established in the headings in conformity with Library of Congress rules of cataloguing practice. It has seemed permissible, therefore, to keep those Royal princesses of Great Britain who married beneath them in rank, as well as their husbands, under their given names, as royalty, following Library of Congress, and thus deviating from the accepted genealogical authority, the Almanach de Gotha. Below the heading, the "inscription" or lettering transcribed from the bookplate, exclusive of motto or text not essential to identification, is quoted in capitals. "Anonymous" is supplied when name, initial, or "cipher" is absent, regardless of whether or not the identity of the owner has been established.

"Unsigned" has been used only when the name of the artist which follows has been supplied from some other source than the bookplate itself. Size is given in inches. Three dots indicate an omission in headings which repeat the entry preceding. This may be observed in particular for the Windsor Castle bookplates and the gift of George I to Cambridge University, a series in which designs have been created in folio, quarto, and octavo to be inserted in volumes of a corresponding size.

To Miss Lucy E. Osborne, Custodian of the Chapin Library of Williams College, I am indebted for assistance on many counts, not the least of which is the checking of the volumes of the *"Ex Libris. Buchkunst und Angewandte Graphik"* in the New York Public Library. I am grateful to Mr. Nicholas R. Rodionoff, Chief of the Slavic Division of the Library of Congress for his report on certain Russian bookplates. From my own department in the University of California Library I wish to record my thanks to Mrs. Gerda F.

Behrens, who has interpreted the text of the Slavic inscriptions, while Miss Margaret N. White, specialist in history, and Homer Rutherford, student assistant, with a flair for genealogy and heraldry, have both responded with the answers to a variety of queries in their particular fields.

C. P.

Berkeley, California
October 18, 1942

Great Britain

1 Royal Body Guard of the King, "G v R", St. James's Palace.

"HIS MAJESTY'S BODY GUARD OF THE HON. CORPS OF GENTLEMEN AT ARMS"

Pictorial armorial. View of the gateway to St. James's Palace, bordered by the king's and the regimental colors. The royal arms below, and above a portcullis with chains pendant for the City of Westminster, ensigned by a crown.

Engraving, signed and dated: W.P.B. (Barrett) 1911. Proof. 6⅞x5⅝.

2 James I, 1566-1625. *(As James VI of Scotland).*

"R I 6"

Full armorial, with unicorn supporters, bearing the banners of Scotland (dexter) and St. Andrew (sinister). The lion "rampant" of Scotland on a shield, surrounded by the collar of the Order of the Thistle, with the badge attached. Motto: In defense.

Engraving. [ca. 1580-1590] 9⅜x6⅜

As sovereigns of England, the Stuarts bore the British arms as represented on the shield of Charles II, Plate VIII.

3 Cambridge. University. Library. (Gift plate for the library of John Moore, Bishop of Ely, donated by George I).

"MVNIFICENTIA REGIA. 1715"

Armorial, allegorical. Arms of the University in a frame with escalloped border, decorated with a cherub's head. On an architectural base, with books, in the center of which is inserted a medallion portrait of the King, reading round its exergue: GEORGIVS D. G. MAG. BR. FR. ET HIB. REX F.D.

Engraving, signed: J. Pine, Sculp. [1736-37] 2⅞x2¼   Plate II.

For this great donation of 28,965 printed books and 1,790 manuscripts, John Pine was commissioned to execute plates in four sizes. The three largest are alike in design (no. 4, 6, 7), no. 3 omits the symbolic figures and pyramid. No. 5 is a copy by another hand.

4 Cambridge. University. Library . . .
"MVNIFICENTIA REGIA. 1715"

The University arms within an oval shield, at either side of which are posed the figures of Apollo and Minerva. In the background is a pyramid partly hidden amid clouds and rays, while the whole rests on a base as above.

Engraving, signed: J.P., Sc. [1736-37] 3⅝x2⅞ (Octavo plate)

5 Cambridge. University. Library . . .
"MVNIFICENTIA REGIA. 1715"

Copy of design above.

Signed: J.B. Sc. (Copy of the plate by Pine, executed by John Baldrey) [ca. 1790] 3⅞x3⅜

6 Cambridge. University. Library . . .
"MVNIFICENTIA REGIA. 1715"

Design as above.

Signed: J.P. Sc. [1736-37] 5⅜x4⅜ (Quarto plate)

7 Cambridge. University. Library . . .
"MVNIFICENTIA REGIA. 1715"

Design as above.

Signed: J. Pine Sculp. [1736-37] 9⅛x7¼ (Folio plate)

8 George III, 1738-1820.
[ANONYMOUS]

Chippendale armorial, allegorical. The royal shield, crown, and mantle are borne aloft by cherubs, while the figure of Fame sounds a trumpet.

Engraving, signed: F. Bartolozzi Inv:Sculp. [ca.1780] 9½x12

A supposed design for a bookplate, or possibly intended for the title-page of a folio volume.

9 Windsor Castle. Royal Library. Queen Victoria, 1819-1901.
"V R I ROYAL LIBRARY, WINDSOR CASTLE"

Armorial. Royal crest of England: Upon the imperial crown, a lion, "statant guardant," imperially crowned. "V R I" above, Royal Library, etc. below on a ribbon.

Etching, signed: G.W.E. (Eve; in monogram) [1898] 4¾x3⅞ (Octavo plate) Eve no. 54.

Plate 1

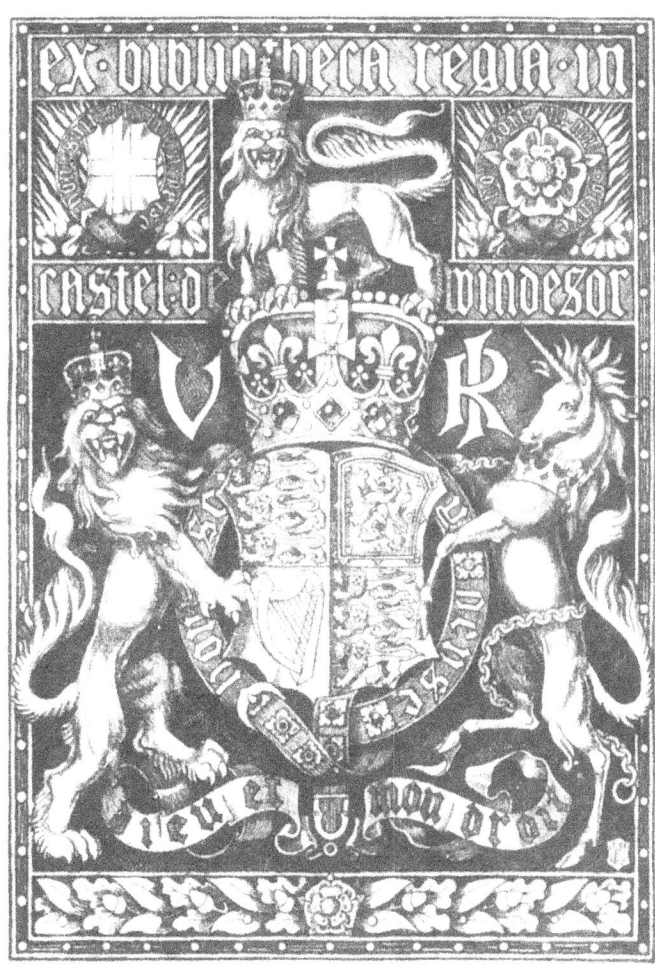

10   Windsor Castle. Royal Library . . .

"ROYAL LIBRARY V R I WINDSOR CASTLE"

Armorial. The royal arms encircled by the Garter and surmounted by an imperial crown. With the emblematic rose, thistle, and shamrock. "Royal Library" and cipher above, "Windsor Castle" below.

Etching, signed and dated: G.W.E. (Eve; in monogram) '97. 5¾x4½ (Quarto plate) Eve no. 41.

11   Windsor Castle. Royal Library . . .

"EX BIBLIOTHECA REGIA IN CASTEL DE WINDESOR V R I"

Full armorial. Arms as no. 10 and crest as no. 9, with the addition of supporters and two upper compartments which display the badges of St. George and the Tudor rose over the "sun-burst" badge of Edward III, symbolical of the fact that Windsor is the special home of the Knights of the Garter. Below is a band of oak and laurel leaves placed alternately, with the Tudor rose in the center. Inscription above.

Etching, signed and dated: G.W.E. (Eve; in monogram) 1898. 7x4¾ (Folio plate) Eve. no. 53.   Plate I.

12   Victoria, Queen, 1819-1901.

"V R HER MAJESTY'S PRIVATE LIBRARY, BUCKINGHAM PALACE"

Armorial. The royal cipher, the initials "V R" bound together by a looped cord and set within the Garter. Ensigned with the royal crown. "Case" and "shelf" indicated above; inscription below.

Engraving. [1860] 3⅞x2½

Queen Victoria was the first woman to wear the Garter, which she did by virtue of birth, while Queen Alexandra was the first woman on whom the Order was bestowed (by Edward VII).

13   Albert, Prince Consort of Queen Victoria, 1819-1861.

"H.R.H. ALBERT. PRINCE CONSORT"

Portrait. With maxim below: Always labouring for the good of others. Initials "V" and "R" in lower corner compartments.

Engraving. [1865] 2¾x1¾

Indicated as a memorial plate by the tribute and assigned date.

14   Albert, Prince Consort . . .

[ANONYMOUS]

Armorial, with supporters. The shield: quarterly, 1 and 4, royal arms as borne by Queen Victoria, differenced by a label of three points, charged at the center point with a cross; 2 and 3, Saxony. Encircled by the Garter, and ensigned with the Prince's own coronet. Motto: Treu und Fest.

Engraving [ca. 1850] 1⅝x2

15 Albert, Prince Consort . . .

[ANONYMOUS]

Armorial, with supporters. Arms and motto as above.

Reproduced from an engraving, signed: M. Byfield (Mary Byfield) Sc. 3⅛x3⅞

16 Windsor Castle. Royal Library. Edward VII, 1841-1910.

"EX BIBLIOTHECA REGIA IN CASTEL DE WINDESOR E R"

Full armorial, with supporters. A reworking of no. 11 above, with "E R" substituted for "V R I" and other slight variations.

Etching, signed and dated: G.W.E., 1898 (original date unchanged) [1902] Sepia. (Folio plate) Proof, autographed: Geo. W. Eve. With remarque (the Union badge) lettered: K.E.H.F. (King Edward's hospital fund) 11x7¾ Eve. no. 88. Cf. Plate I.

Of this variety, proof form and bearing the remarque, fifty prints each were struck for nos. 16, 17 and 18.

17 Windsor Castle. Royal Library . . .

"ROYAL LIBRARY E R WINDSOR CASTLE"

Armorial, a reworking of no. 10 above, with a substitution of initials, and slight variations in decoration.

Etching, signed and dated: G.W.E. (in monogram) '97 (original date unchanged) [1902] Sepia. (Quarto plate) Proof, autographed: Geo. W. Eve. With remarque, etc. as no. 16 above. 11x7¾ Eve no. 87.

18 Windsor Castle. Royal Library . . .

"E R ROYAL LIBRARY, WINDSOR CASTLE"

The royal crest, a reworking of no. 9 above, with a substitution of initials, and shading added to scroll.

Etching, signed: G.W.E. [1902] Sepia. (Octavo plate) Proof, autographed: Geo. W. Eve. With remarque (not lettered), otherwise as no. 16-17 above. 11x7¾ Eve no. 89.

19 Alexandra House. Queen Alexandra, 1844-1925.

"ALEXANDRA HOUSE, KENSINGTON GORE. 1884"

Portrait. The Queen's portrait, set within a frame designed in the form of the badge of the Tudor rose. Cipher below.

Lithograph. [1884] 4⅛x2⅞   Plate II.

20 Alexandra, Queen Consort of Edward VII, 1844-1925. *(While Princess of Wales). Born Princess of Denmark.*

"ALEXANDRA"

Pictorial. In two compartments, each with a landscape, the whole framed in a border of oak leaves and roses. In the lower panel Castle Elsinore, early home of the Danish princess; above, Windsor Castle. Personal tastes are suggested in the music, books and dogs which form details in the design. The badge of three ostrich feathers is placed within the border. Name below.

Engraving, signed: W.P.B. (Barrett) [ca. 1900?—before 1901] Proof. 6⅝x5¼

21 Windsor Castle. Royal Library. George V, 1865-1936.

"G V R EX BIBLIOTHECA REG. IN CASTEL WINDESOR"
Armorial. The royal arms encircled by the Garter, and surmounted by a royal crown. Design resembling nos. 10 and 17 above, but with inscription similar to the folio plate of the series, i.e. nos. 11 and 16.

Etching, signed and dated: G. W. E. (Eve). 1911. Sepia. 5⅛x4 (Quarto plate) Eve. no. 197.

22 George V, 1865-1936. *(While Prince of Wales).*

"THE LIBRARY OF GEORGE FREDERICK ERNEST ALBERT, PRINCE OF WALES"

Full armorial, with supporters and mantling. Royal arms, with an escutcheon of pretence for Saxony, differenced by a label, and surrounded by the Garter. In upper compartments, badges: the plume of three ostrich feathers of the heir apparent, and the dragon for Wales. Below, the Prince of Wale's motto: Ich dien, and anchors at either side of the name. In upper corners, the Tudor rose.

Engraving, signed and dated: Inv W.P.B. (Barrett) 1904. Proof. 7⅞x6¾   Plate VI.

23 Mary, Queen Consort of George V, 1867-   *Born Princess of Teck.*

"MARY"

Decorative armorial. The name is inscribed upon a tablet set within a floral frame, richly decorated in a motif of rose, thistle, and shamrock. Above, the royal crown upheld by two cherubs.

Engraving, signed: W.P.B. (Barrett) Pencilled date: 1910. Proof. 7¼x5¾

24 George V and Queen Mary. *(While Duke and Duchess of of York. "The Wedding Ex Libris").*

"GEORGE & MARY," and within border compartments: "EX-LIBRIS. YORK. TECK"

Full armorial, with supporters. An elaborate design, showing two heart-shaped shields, accollé at center, and below a label charged with a cross, anchor, and heart, with lettering, "Faith, Hope, Charity."

Reproduction from an original drawing, signed and dated: John Leighton F.S.A. July 1893. Manuscript note: First motif. 7½x7

25 George V and Queen Mary . . .

"GEORGE & MARY"

Design as above, with a ribbon bearing the inscription: Jul. & Aug. Exhibit at the Imperial Ins. (Institute) A.D. 1893.

Signed and dated as above. Manuscript note: Second motif. 6½x6⅜

26 George V and Queen Mary . . .

"GEORGE & MARY"

Design as above, with inscribed ribbon.

Signed and dated. Manuscript note: Third motif. 7⅜x7¼

27 George V and Queen Mary . . .

"GEORGE & MARY"

Design as above, without inscribed ribbon.

Signed and dated. Manuscript note: Coloured motif (in yellow, rose, and white). 7¼x6⅜

28 George V and Queen Mary . . .

"GEORGE & MARY"

Design as above, without inscribed ribbon.

Signed and dated. Manuscript note: Original drawing on blue board. 10x8¾

Plate ii

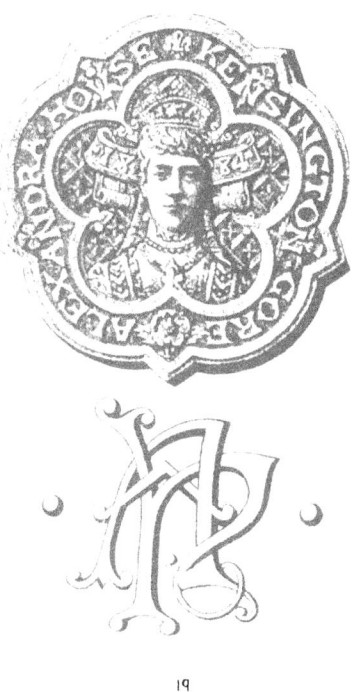

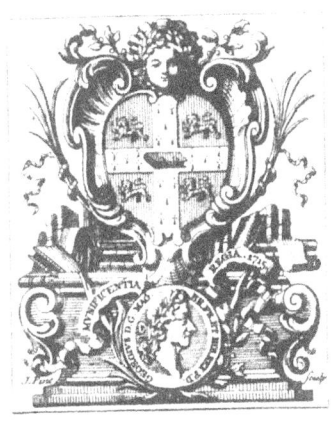

19

3

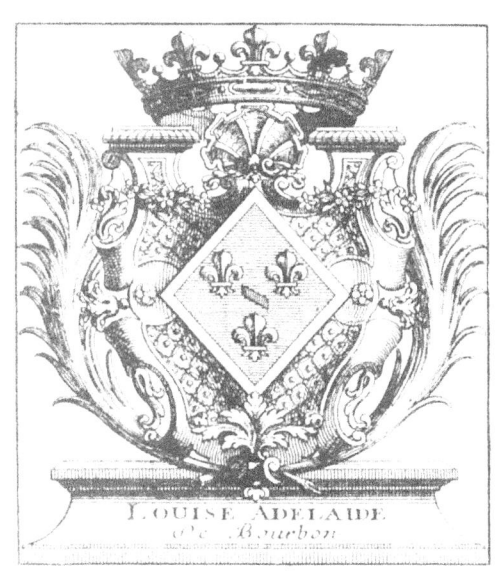

119

109

29 Edward, Duke of Windsor, 1894-   *(While Prince of Wales). Renounced the throne as Edward VIII, 1936.*

"E"

Decorative armorial. The initial on a cartouche, with a decorative border of intertwined rose, thistle, and shamrock, ensigned with a princely coronet.

Engraving, signed and dated: Inv. W.P.B. (Barrett) 1904. Proof. 10x7¼

30 Charles I, 1600-1649.

"CHARLES I R"

Full armorial, with supporters and mantling. Text below arms as follows: Haueing caused this Translation of the Psalmes (whereof oure late deare Father was Author) to be perused, and it being found to be exactly and truely done wee doe hereby authorize the same to be Imprinted according to the Patent graunted thereupon, and doe allow them to be song in all the Churches of oure Dominiones recommending them to all oure goode Subjects for that effect.

Engraving, signed: Will. Marshall. Sculpsit. [ca. 1630] 5⅜x3¼

"This is not a true bookplate . . . It was placed either on the covers, or the verso of the title pages, of the 1630 edition of King James I translation of the Psalms . . ." (From printed annotation accompanying plate)

31 Kapurthala, Sir Jagatjit Singh, Hereditary Maharajah of, 1872-

"J S"

Armorial. Crest (a sword) ensigned with a crown, and the monogram below.

Engraving, in gold, on vellum. Date assigned in album: 1900. 4½x3¾

Sir Jagatjit Singh was a Knight Grand Commander of the Order of the Star of India, 1911.

32 Kapurthala . . .

[ANONYMOUS]

Full armorial, with elephant and unicorn supporters. Shield in blue and white, on a mantle bordered with red, and surmounted by a crown and crest in gold. Motto: Pro rege et patria.

Engraving, in gold and colors, on vellum. Date assigned in album: 1900. 7½x4⅝

33 Windsor Castle. Royal Library. George VI, 1893-

"G VI R ROYAL LIBRARY, WINDSOR CASTLE"

Pictorial armorial. Saint George on horseback encountering the dragon, encircled by the Garter, and ensigned with the royal cipher. Inscription below.

Etching and engraving, unsigned. [By Stephen Gooden, 1937] Sepia. 6⅛x4⅛ (Quarto plate)

Ordered in 1936, this plate was completed with the cipher "E R" and about fifty copies inserted in books before the abdication of Edward VIII. The two remaining plates in the series (nos. 34-35) were engraved with the initials "G VI R" at the beginning.

34 Windsor Castle. Royal Library ...

"G VI R ROYAL LIBRARY, WINDSOR CASTLE"

Full armorial, with supporters. The royal arms within the Garter, drawn on a richly sculptured panel, with the emblematic rose, thistle, and shamrock below. Inscription on a tablet forming the base.

Etching and engraving, unsigned. [By Stephen Gooden, 1937] Sepia. 7¾x5 (Folio plate)

35 Windsor Castle. Royal Library ...

"ROYAL LIBRARY, WINDSOR CASTLE. G VI R"

Decorative armorial. A "leopard's" head, crowned, within an oval frame. Inscription around the border.

Etching and engraving, unsigned. [By Stephen Gooden, 1937] Sepia. 3½x3 (Octavo plate)

36 George VI, 1893-   (*While Duke of York*).

"A" (Albert Fredrick Arthur George)

Decorative armorial. Identical with the plate of Edward, Prince of Wales (no. 29) except that the cipher "A" replaces the "E", and is without shading.

Engraving, signed and dated: Inv. W.P.B. (Barrett) 1904. Proof. 10x7¼

37 Elizabeth, Queen Consort of George VI, 1900-   (*While Duchess of York*).

"ELIZABETH DUCHESS OF YORK"

Decorative amorial. Two ovals accollé, for the Duke and Duchess of York, ensigned with the coronet of rank. On a rich background,

Plate iii

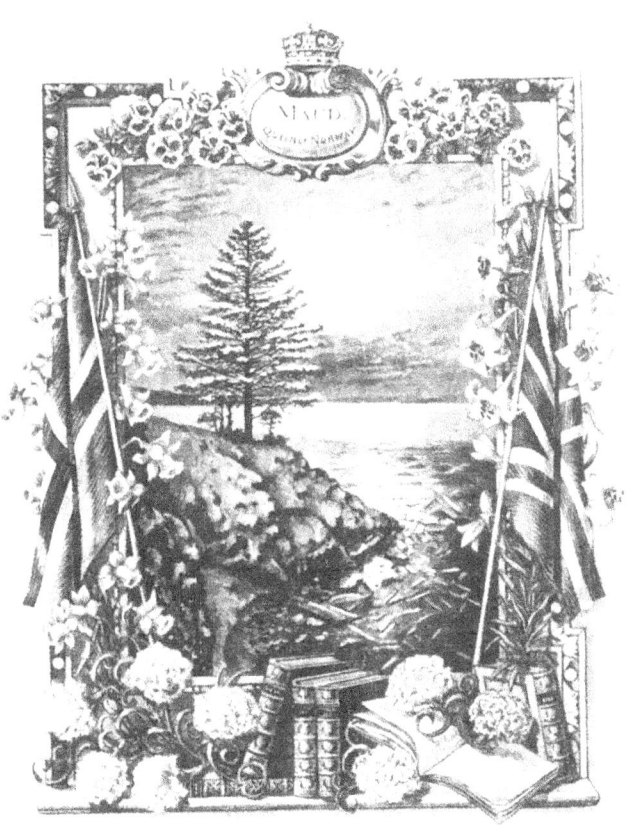

with rose, thistle, and conventional foliage. Name inscribed on a ribbon.

Engraving, signed and dated: W.P.B. (Barrett) 1925. Proof. 7¼x5¾

38 Henry, Duke of Gloucester, 1900-   *Third son of George V.*

"H - GLOUCESTER"

Decorative armorial. The initial "H" set within the Garter and ensigned with the coronet of rank; "Gloucester" below.

Engraving, unsigned. [By W. P. Barrett] 4½x3½

39 Alice, Countess of Athlone, 1883-   *Born Princess of Great Britain. Eldest daughter of Prince Leopold, Duke of Albany, fourth son of Queen Victoria.*

"ALICE MARY VICTORIA AUGUSTA PAULINE"

Armorial. The royal arms, with an escutcheon of pretence for Saxony, on an oval within a ribbon bearing the name, and surmounted by the coronet of rank. Festooned border decoration.

Engraving [ca. 1895?] Light buff. 3⅞x2½

The Princess Alice married Prince Alexander of Teck, who renounced his German title in 1917 and was created Earl of Athlone.

40 Louise, Duchess of Fife, 1867-1931. *Born Princess Royal of Great Britain. Eldest daughter of Edward VII.*

[ANONYMOUS]

Armorial lozenge, with supporters. The royal arms differenced by a label of five points charged with two thistles between three crosses, and an escutcheon of pretence for Saxony. Surmounted by a coronet of rank.

Engraving. [Before her marriage in 1889] 6¼x4½

The arms of Saxony on the small shield of pretence (from the arms of the Prince Consort) were borne on the paternal arms only up to 1901, when the Prince of Wales ascended the throne as Edward VII.

41 Maud, Queen Consort of Haakon VII, King of Norway, 1869-1938. *Third daughter of Edward VII.*

"MAUD, QUEEN OF NORWAY"

Pictorial. View of a moonlit shore, with border decoration introducing Norwegian and English flags, flowers, and books. Name above on a cartouche, ensigned with a crown.

Engraving, signed and dated: Inv. W.P.B. (Barrett) 1907. Proof.
7x5   Plate III.

42 Victoria, Princess, 1868-1935. *Second daughter of Edward VII.*

"VICTORIA"

Pictorial. View of a lonely coast at night, with crescent moon, cross, dove, and the score of *Lohengrin*. Decorative leafy border of oak and laurel.

Engraving, signed and dated: Inv. W.P.B. (Barrett) 1900. Proof.
7⅜x5¾

43 Mary, Countess of Harewood, 1897-   *Born Princess Royal of Great Britain. Only daughter of George V.*

"M"

Decorative armorial. A reduced design of no. 29, with "M" at center.

Engraving, signed and dated: W.P.B. (Barrett) 1910. Proof. 6x4⅞

44 Mary, Queen Consort of George V, 1867-   "Doll's House."

"M R I EX LIBRIS"

Miniature armorial. The Queen's cipher ensigned with a royal crown. "Ex libris" below.

Engraving, unsigned. [By W. P. Barrett] Proof. 4½x3½

45 Louisa Margaret, Duchess of Connaught, 1860-1917. *Born Princess of Prussia. Consort of Arthur, Duke of Connaught, third son of Queen Victoria.*

"L M"

Festoon. Monogram within a beaded oval, bordered by sprays of palm and laurel. Ensigned with a coronet of rank, and set within a festooned frame.

Engraving, signed and dated: Inv. W.P.B. (Barrett) 1905. 4¼x3¼
                                                              Plate IV.

46 Louisa Margaret . . .

"L M"

Design as above.

Proof. 9⅜x6½

Plate iv

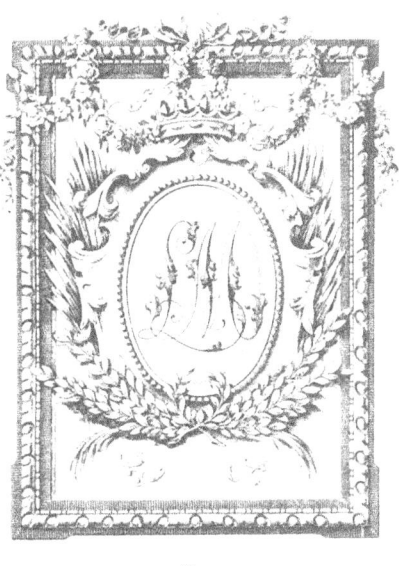

45

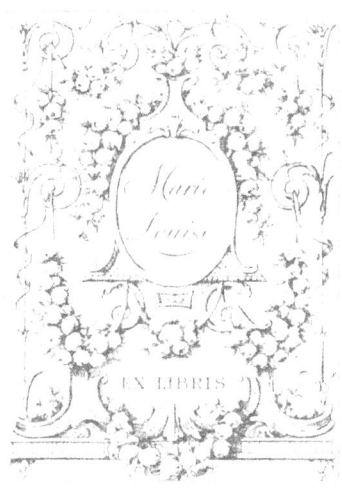

154

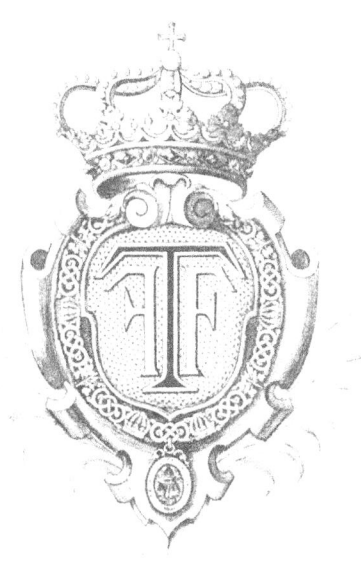

47

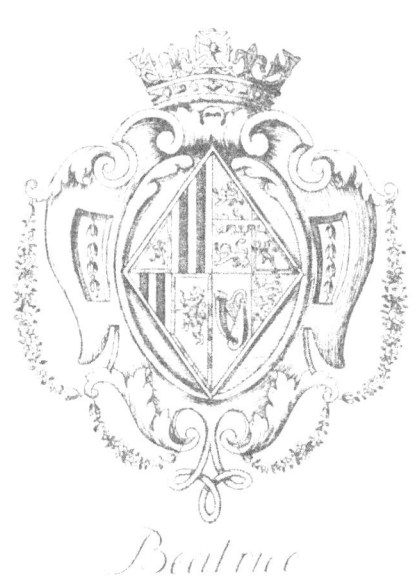

51

47 Francis, Prince and Duke of Teck, 1837-1900. *Father of Queen Mary.*

"F T F"

Armorial. Initials on a cartouche surrounded by the collar, with the pendant badge, of the Order of the Bath, with its motto, "Tria juncta in uno." Sprays of palm below; above, a crown.

Engraving, signed and dated: C. W. Sherborn R E fecit 1896. 4x3
Plate IV.

48 Mary, Queen Consort of George V, 1867-   (*While Princess "May," Duchess of York*).

"V M" (Victoria Mary)
Decorative armorial. The monogram upon a cartouche is bordered by sprays of "May" blossoms, and surmounted by the coronet of rank.

Engraving, signed: C. W. Sherborn, Sc. [ca. 1890] 4x3

49 Mary Adelaide, Duchess of Teck, 1833-1897. *Born Princess of Great Britain. Daughter of Adolphus, Duke of Cambridge, seventh son of George III. Mother of Queen Mary.*

"M A"

Decorative armorial. The monogram upon a cartouche is set within a carved frame, bordered by palm branches, the coronet of rank above.

Engraving, signed and dated: C. W. Sherborn ft. 1890. 4x3

50 Helena, Princess Christian of Schleswig-Holstein, 1846-1923. *Third daughter of Queen Victoria.*

"HELENA"

Pictorial, showing a residence (probably Cumberland House, Windsor). In the foreground is seen an interior indicating literary and musical tastes, with a border panel enclosing a bouquet of the symbolic rose, thistle, and shamrock. Above this, the name on a cartouche, surmounted by the coronet of rank. Motto: Steadfast and true.

Engraving, unsigned. [By F. G. House? 1906?] Proof. 6⅝x5¼

51 Beatrice, Princess Henry of Battenberg, 1857- *Youngest daughter of Queen Victoria.*

"BEATRICE"

Armorial lozenge. Arms of Hesse, impaled with the arms of Britain, differenced by a label of three points, the center charged with a heart and each of the others with a rose. Within a heavily-lined frame, festoons depending from the sides, and ensigned with the coronet of rank. Name below.

Etching, signed and dated: J.F.B. (Badeley) 1928. 4⅛x3⅛.
Plate IV.

52 Henry, Prince of Battenberg, 1858-1896. *Married the Princess Beatrice.*

"FÜRSTLICH BATTENBERGSCHE BIBLIOTHEK"

Seal armorial. Arms of Hesse, with two crests for Hesse and Battenberg. Ensigned with a crown. Motto: In te Domine spero. Inscription within border.

Engraving, signed: A. & C. Downey. [1890] 3¼x2⅜

A plate also used by other members of the House of Battenberg.

53 Carisbrooke, Alexander Albert Mountbatten, 1st Marquis of, 1886-   Formerly Prince of Battenberg. *Son of Prince Henry of Battenberg and the Princess Beatrice.*

"EX LIBRIS ALEXANDER MOUNTBATTEN, FIRST MARQUESS OF CARISBROOKE"

Full armorial, bearing on the shield, 1 and 4, the royal arms as borne by Queen Victoria, differenced by a label charged with a heart and two roses; 2 and 3, arms of Hesse within a bordure. Above, crests for Hesse and Battenberg. Motto: In te Domine spero. On a tablet at the base, the name.

Engraving, signed in monogram (unidentified). Sepia. 5¾x4¼

54 Milford Haven, George Mountbatten, 2d Marquis of, 1892-1938. Formerly Prince of Battenberg. *Eldest son of the 1st Marquis and Princess Victoria of Hesse, eldest daughter of Alice 2d daughter of Queen Victoria.*

"GEORGE, 2d MARQUESS OF MILFORD HAVEN, ROYAL NAVY"

Full armorial, with supporters. The paternal arms (lions of Hesse) charged at the honor point with an escutcheon of the arms as borne by the late Princess Alice, namely the royal arms differenced by a label of three points, the center point charged with a rose and each of the other points with an ermine spot. Surrounded by the collar of the Royal Victorian Order, with the badge of the Order depending. Crests of Hesse and Battenberg. Motto: In honour bound. Inscription below.

Engraving, signed and dated: A Batchelor F, London, 1927. 5⅜x3¾.
Plate VI.

55 Milford Haven, George Mountbatten . . . (*While Earl of Medina*).

"GEORGE, EARL OF MEDINA. ROYAL NAVY"

Armorial. The legend is inscribed around an oval frame, enclosing the arms as no. 54 above. Bordered by flags of the Royal Navy, and ensigned with the coronet of rank. Above, on a ribbon "MOUNT-BATTEN" and the crest of Hesse.

Etching. [1917-21] Sepia. 3⅞x3½

56 Mountbatten, Lord Louis, 1900-   *Second son of the 1st Marquis of Milford Haven and Princess Victoria of Hesse.*

"LORD LOUIS MOUNTBATTEN. ROYAL NAVY"

Armorial. Arms, with supporters. Encircled by the collar of the Royal Victorian Order, etc. as no. 54.

Engraving, signed and dated: A. Batchelor, F. London, 1923. 4⅝x3½

57 Victoria, Princess, 1868-1935. *Second daughter of Edward VII.*

"VICTORIA"

Proof on cream paper of no. 42. 9⅛x7⅞

58 Henry VIII, 1491-1547, and Katharine of Aragon, Queen Consort, 1485-1536.

"H K"

Decorative armorial. A leafy stem bearing on the dexter side the Tudor rose, and on the sinister the cleft pomegranate of Aragon, ensigned with the royal crown. Bordered by the initials "H" and "K" interlaced with a cord.

Engraving. 5⅝x3⅞   Plate V.

59 James I, 1566-1625.

[ANONYMOUS]

Decorative armorial. A Tudor rose ensigned with a royal crown.

Engraving. 3½x2⅝   Plate V.

Assigned to James I in the collection, but quite possibly the mark of Queen Elizabeth, who used a similar motif on her bookbindings, while King James combined the rose and thistle. Obviously an old plate, but it is to be recalled that the badge of the Tudor rose for England has been employed since Henry VII (1455-1509)

60 George III, 1738-1820.

"G III R"

Armorial. The royal arms within the Garter, on a mantle. Inscription above the crown.

Engraving. 3⅛x2¾   Plate XII.

George III formed a magnificent library, which was presented to the British Museum, in accordance with an arrangement made with the Treasury, by George IV in 1823.

61 Charlotte, Queen Consort of George III, 1744-1818. *Born Princess of Mecklenburg-Strelitz.*

"S" (Sophia Charlotte)

Armorial. The initial, drawn upon a lined background within a beaded oval, is surmounted by a crown.

Engraving. 2⅜x1⅝

62 Charlotte, Queen Consort . . .

[ANONYMOUS]

Armorial. Arms of Great Britain and Mecklenburg-Strelitz impaled; on a mantle. Surmounted by a crown, with border decoration of festooned leaves and flowers.

Engraving. 3½ square.

63 William IV, 1765-1837.

"W R IIII"

Armorial. The royal cipher within the Garter, ensigned with a crown.

Engraving. [ca. 1830] 3x4¼

64 George IV, 1762-1830. *(While Prince of Wales)* and Frederick, Duke of York and Albany, 1763-1827.

"PRINCE OF WALES AND THE BISHOP OF OSNABURGH, 3rd MAY, 1771"

Armorial. Inscription on a ribbon, encircling both the "Prince of Wales's feathers" (the triple ostrich plume) and the royal crest, differenced with a coronet and a label of three points charged at the center point with a cross, for Prince Frederick.

Engraving, signed: J. Kirk sculpt. Bedford Str. Covt. Garden. 1771. 2x3¼

Plate v

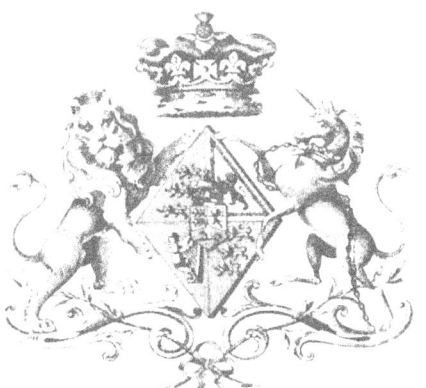

Elizabeth.

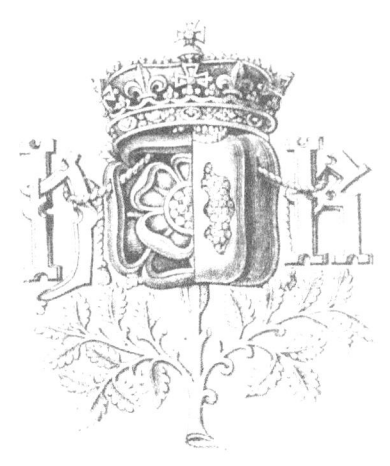

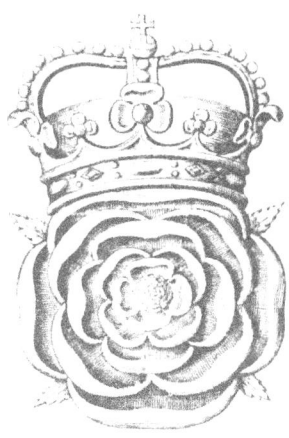

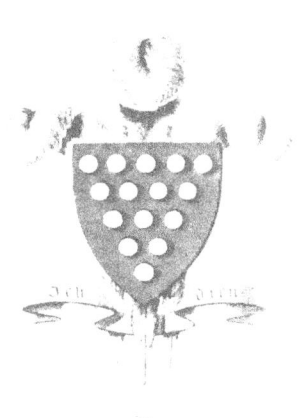

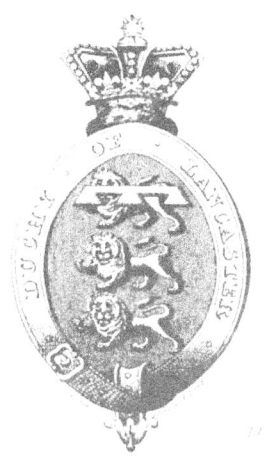

This plate is supposed to have been intended for the school books of the two eldest sons of George III. The young Prince Frederick was elected titular bishop of Osnabrück in 1764.

65 George IV, 1762-1830. *(While Prince of Wales).*
"THE PRINCE OF WALES'S LIBRARY"

Full armorial, with supporters. The royal arms differenced with a label, within the Garter and surrounded by the collar of the Order of the Garter, depending from which is the "Great George," and badges of the Order of the Golden Fleece and one other, unidentified. Above, the royal crest and the badge of the heir apparent with the motto, "Ich dien" on a ribbon. Inscription below.

Engraving. 4⅜x3⅛

66 George IV, 1762-1830.
"G. IV. R. ROYAL LIBRARY"

Full armorial. Royal arms, with supporters, within the Garter and surrounded by the collar of the Order of the Garter, depending from which is the badge of the "Great George." Upon a mantle. Inscription below.

Engraving, signed: Silvester Sc. 27, Strand. [ca. 1820] 4¼x3.

Plate XII.

67 Elizabeth, Consort of Friedrich VI, Landgrave of Hesse-Homburg, 1770-1840. *Third daughter of George III.*
"ELIZABETH"

Armorial lozenge. Arms of Great Britain, as borne by George III, with supporters. Ensigned with the coronet of rank. Name below.

Engraving. 3½x2½   Plate V.

A plate used before her marriage (1818).

68 Augustus Frederick, Duke of Sussex, 1773-1843. *Sixth son of George III.*
[ANONYMOUS]

Full armorial, with supporters. The royal arms differenced with a label of three points, charged at the center point with two hearts between a cross at either end, within the Garter, and surrounded by the collar of the Order of the Garter with the "George" depending. Motto: Si Deus pro nobis quis contra nos.

Engraving. [ca. 1825] 4⅛x3⅜

31

69 Augustus Frederick . . .

[ANONYMOUS]

Design as above, with the addition of a bracket.

Engraving, signed: Perkins and Heath, patent hardened steel plate.
4½x3⅜

70 William Frederick, 2d Duke of Gloucester and Edinburgh,
1776-1834. *Great grandson of George II.*

[ANONYMOUS]

Full armorial, with supporters. Royal arms differenced with a label
of five points charged with a fleur-de-lis at center, and four crosses.
Encircled by the Order of the Garter.

Engraving. [ca. 1805] 3½ square.

71 Augustus Frederick, Duke of Sussex, 1773-1843. *See no. 68.*

[ANONYMOUS]

Pictorial armorial. The royal crest within the collar of the Order of
the Garter. A helmet, an owl and the "George," with a spray of
leaves form a frame for the book number at the base.

Engraving, signed: Perkins and Heath . . . [ca. 1825] 3⅞x2½

72 George II, 1683-1760.

"R A G" (Rex George Augustus) ?

Monogram armorial. A cipher within the Garter, surmounted by a
crown.

Engraving. 3¾x2⅝

Although unable to identify this plate definitely, I do not believe it
to have belonged to "Henry styled 'William Henry' Duke of
Gloucester, son [i.e. brother] of George III" as marked in the collection. The "R" and crown would indicate a sovereign. The middle
letter though like an old-fashioned "A" might also be an "H".

The "Old Royal Library," including manuscripts and printed books
collected by British sovereigns from Henry VII to George II, was
presented by the latter to the British Museum in 1757.

73 William Frederick, 2d Duke of Gloucester and Edinburgh,
1776-1834. *See no. 70.*

"W F"

Monogram armorial. Initials within the Garter, surmounted by a
coronet of rank, and set within an oval frame.

Engraving. [ca. 1800] 3¾x2⅝

Plate vi

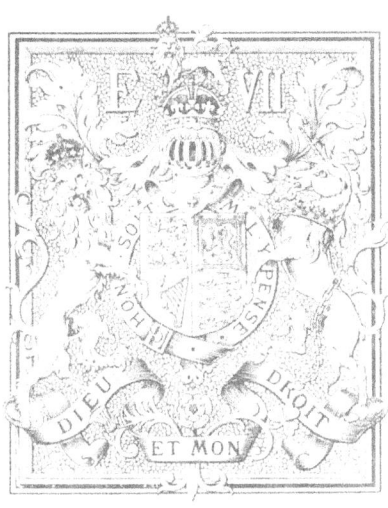

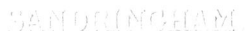

87

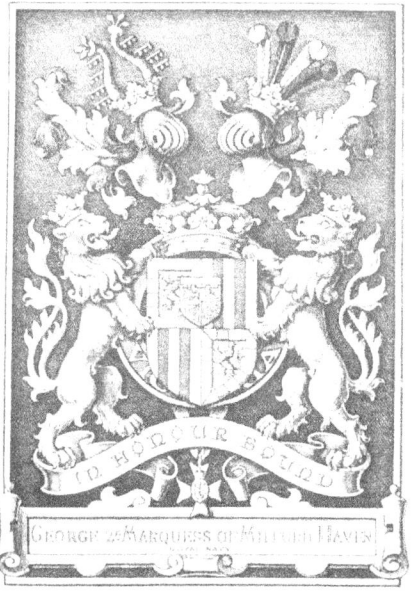

54

85

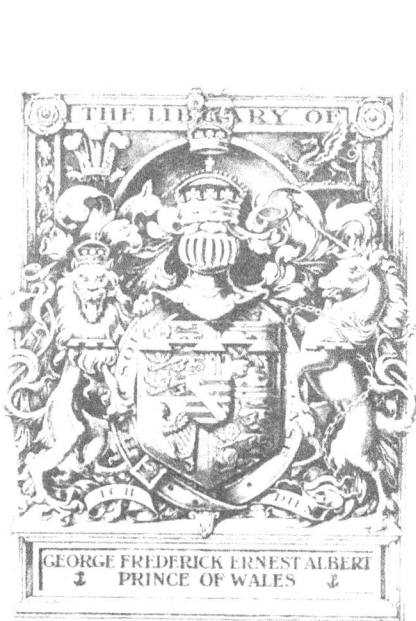

22

74 Sophia, Princess of Great Britain, 1777-1848. *Fifth daughter of George III.*

"H R H PRINCESS SOPHIA"

Decorative armorial. The inscription is enclosed in a wreath, and ensigned with a coronet.

Engraving. [ca. 1820] 3⅛x2½

75 George, 2d Duke of Cambridge, 1819-1904. *Grandson of George III.*

"GEORGE, PRINCE OF CAMBRIDGE"

Full armorial, with supporters. The royal arms differenced with two labels, both of three points. The upper label is charged with two hearts each, dexter and sinister, and a cross at center, which is the label of the first Duke of Cambridge; the lower label is plain. Within the Garter and surrounded by the collar of the Order, with the "George". On a bracket. Inscription below.

Engraving. [ca. 1860] 3⅞x3

Although styled "Prince George," (of Cambridge), it still seems possible that the 2nd Duke in his father's lifetime, and even after, might have been known as the "Prince of Cambridge."

76 Cornwall, Duchy of. *(A royal duchy).*

[ANONYMOUS]

Armorial. A shield spotted with roundels, over the badge of the heir apparent, the triple plume. With the motto: "Ich dien" on a ribbon.

Engraving. 2⅝x2¼   Plate V.

The library of the Duchy of Cornwall was founded by George, Prince of Wales (later George IV) in 1783. This is possibly a plate made for Albert Edward, Prince of Wales (later Edward VII) who became at his birth Duke of Cornwall.

77 Lancaster, Duchy of. *(A royal duchy).*

"DUCHY OF LANCASTER"

Armorial. The three lions of England on a shield, differenced with a label, and encircled by a garter bearing the inscription. Surmounted by a crown.

Engraving, signed: W. Alexander, sc., 50 Strand, London. 3⅞x2½.
                                                         Plate V.

78 Fitzclarence, Lord Frederick, 1799-1854. Second son of *William IV, while Duke of Clarence, by Dora Bland (Mrs. Jordan)*.

"LORD FREDERICK FITZCLARENCE," with inscription at head of bookplate: This belonged to my father when Duke of Clarence, and was left me by the will of Queen Adelaide.

Full armorial, with supporters. The royal arms debruised by a "baton sinister" charged with a cross between two anchors, and encircled by the collar and motto ("Nec aspera terrent") of the Royal Hanoverian Guelphic Order, with the badge attached. The British lion supported on a cap of maintenance. With motto: Nec timere nec timide, on a ribbon below.

Engraving. 5¾x4¾

Children of this union were entitled to bear the arms of William IV, without the crown of Hanover, and "debruised" as described. The eldest son was created a peer (no. 79) in 1831, while on the younger children was bestowed by royal grant the title and precedency of the younger issue of a marquis. (nos. 78, 80, 81)

79 Munster, George Fitzclarence, Earl of, 1794-1842. *Eldest son of William IV etc. as no. 78.*

"EARL OF MUNSTER. COL. FITZ CLARENCE"

Full armorial, with supporters. The royal arms debruised by a "baton sinister" charged with three anchors, and ensigned with an earl's coronet. Motto: Nec timere nec timide. A small narrow plate, with wide spacing between the two series of lettering.

Engraving. [ca. 1831] 4⅞x2½

80 Fitzclarence, Lord Adolphus, 1802-1856. *Third son of William IV etc. as no 78.*

"ADOLPHUS FITZCLARENCE" (Facsimile of signature)

Full armorial, with supporters. The royal arms with crest as no. 78. The "baton sinister" is charged with an anchor between two roses. Encircled by the collar of the Guelphic Order with the badge of the Order and a second badge, unidentified.

Engraving. 3½x2⅜

81 Fitzclarence, Lord Augustus, 1805-1854. *Fourth son of William IV etc. as no 78.*

"SIGILIUM DOMINI AUGUSTI DE FITZCLARENCE"

Seal armorial. The royal arms, with the "baton sinister" charged

Plate vii

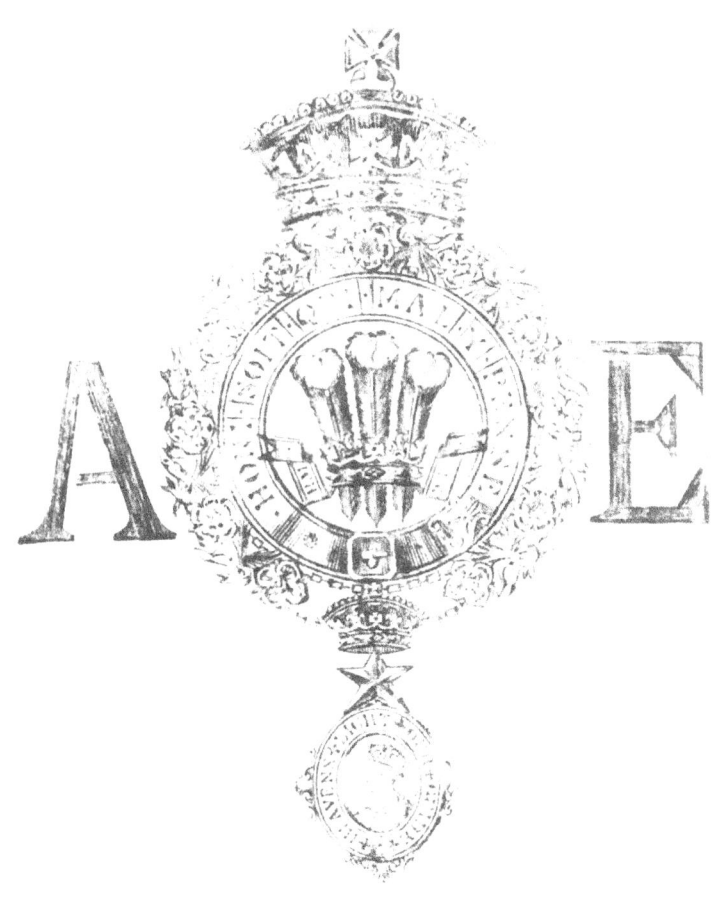

with a cross between two anchors. In seal form, with the inscription around the exergue.

Engraving. [ca. 1840] 5x4⅜

82 Fitzgeorge, Sir Adolphus, 1846-1922. *Second son of George, 2d Duke of Cambridge by his morganatic wife, Louisa Fair-brother (Mrs. Fitzgeorge).*
"SIR ADOLPHUS FITZ-GEORGE"

Armorial, with supporters. Royal arms within the Garter debruised by a "baton sinister," and above, the British lion on a cap of maintenance. On a bracket.

Engraving. 4½x3

83 An adaptation of the royal arms. *(Queen Victoria or later, 1837-).*
[ANONYMOUS]

Armorial, with supporters, a fanciful representation of the British arms, probably stamped upon a bookbinding. Arms within the Garter, with the lion and unicorn bearing upon their backs seated figures carrying cornucopias.

Gold on black cloth. 3¼x2⅜

84 Victoria, Queen, 1819-1901.
"THE QUEEN TO HER ARMY, XMAS 1855"

Label. The inscription within a laurel wreath, surmounted by a crown "in splendor."

Engraving. [1855] 5x3

85 Victoria, Empress Consort of Friedrich III, German Emperor, 1840-1901. *Eldest daughter of Queen Victoria.*
"VICTORIA: A.M.L. (Adelaide Mary Louisa) IMPERATRIX. REGINA"

Armorial. Two shields for Germany and England, surmounted by a crown, with the initials "V" and "F" at either side. On a stippled background decorated with rose, thistle, and shamrock.

Process reproduction, signed: S. (Josef Sattler) [1897] 5½x4½
Plate VI.

Used in the library of the Empress at Castle Cronberg.

86 Edward VII, 1841-1910. *(While Prince of Wales).*
"A E" (Albert Edward)

Decorative armorial. The triple ostrich plume of the heir apparent within the Garter, and surrounded by the collar of the Order of the Star of India, depending from which is the badge of the Order, with its motto, "Heaven's light our guide." Bordered by the initials "A" and "E", and ensigned with the prince's coronet.

Etching. 7¼x4½   Plate VII.

The Most Exalted Order of the Star of India was founded by Queen Victoria in 1861.

87 Edward VII, 1841-1910. Sandringham House.
"E VII," and below: "SANDRINGHAM"

Full armorial, with supporters and mantling. The royal arms encircled by the Garter, upon a background decorated with rose, thistle, and shamrock.

Engraving. Proof. 8¾x7¼   Plate VI.

Sandringham House was acquired by Edward VII, then Prince of Wales, in 1861.

88 George V, 1865-1936.
[ANONYMOUS]

Full armorial, with supporters and mantling. The royal arms within the Garter.

Engraving. 4½x3

89 Edward, Duke of Windsor, 1894-   *(While Prince of Wales). Renounced the throne as Edward VIII, 1936.*
"E"

Pictorial. A library interior, with a book in the foreground displaying on its opened leaves the initial "E" and the badge of the triple ostrich plume. Through an open window a view of a ship under sail.

Etching, signed (in monogram) and dated: MCMXXI. P.T. (Philip Tilden) 7x5½

90 The Royal arms. *(Queen Victoria or later, 1837-   ).*
[ANONYMOUS]

Armorial. With supporters. The royal arms on a Georgian spade shield, within the Garter.

Engraving. 3⅞x2¾

91 Helena Victoria, Princess of Schleswig-Holstein, 1870- *Eldest daughter of Prince Christian of Schleswig-Holstein and the Princess Helena. Cf. no. 50.*

"HELENA VICTORIA"

Armorial lozenge. Quarterly 1 and 4, Great Britain differenced by a label of three points charged with a cross between two roses; (2 and 3) arms for Schleswig-Holstein-Sonderburg-Augustenburg (House of Oldenburg). Framed in a graceful border of acanthus leaves.

Engraving, signed: J.F.B. (Badeley) 4⅛x3⅜

The princely title of Highness was conferred by royal warrant upon children of Prince and Princess Christian, June 30, 1866.

92 Leopold, Duke of Albany, 1853-1884. *Fourth son of Queen Victoria.*

"H.R.H. PRINCE LEOPOLD. K.G."

Full armorial, with supporters. Royal arms differenced with a label of three points charged with a cross between two hearts, and an escutcheon of pretence for Saxony. Three crests for Great Britain, Saxony and Thüringen.

Engraving. 4¾x3

93 The Royal arms. *(Stuart period, 1603-1689, or Queen Anne, 1st period, 1702-1707).*

[ANONYMOUS]

Early armorial, with mantling. Royal arms within the Garter. Set within an oval frame.

Etching. 3¼x2½

Probably not a bookplate.

94 The Royal arms. (Queen Victoria or later, 1837-   ).

[ANONYMOUS]

A highly decorated card, with the royal arms encircled by the Garter. Below, roses and thistles are intertwined with the ribbon bearing the motto.

Process reproduction in gold and colors. 3x4½

Probably not a bookplate.

95 Milford Haven, Louis Alexander Mountbatten, 1st Marquis of, 1854-1921. *Formerly Prince of Battenberg. Married the Princess Victoria. Cf. no. 98.*

"PRINCE LOUIS OF BATTENBERG. ROYAL NAVY"

Decorative armorial. Design within a double square. At center, arms of Hesse differenced by a bordure, surmounted by a crown. Within the upper corner compartments, the crests of Hesse and Battenberg; lower corners, a flag and an anchor. On either side of the shield, badges of the Order of the Bath and Order of the Golden Lion of Hesse-Cassel.

Process reproduction. [Designed by the owner] Sepia. 2 square.

96 Frederick, Duke of York and Albany, 1763-1820. *Second son of George III.*

[ANONYMOUS]

Armorial, with supporters and mantling. Royal arms differenced with a label of three points charged with a cross at center, within the Garter and surrounded by the collar of the Order of the Bath, with depending badge.

Engraving. 4⅜x6

The Order of the Bath was revived by George I in 1725.

97 Charles II, 1630-1685.

[ANONYMOUS]

Early armorial, with supporters and heavy mantling. The royal arms within the Garter. On a bracket, decorated with the emblematic rose and thistle.

Engraving. Dated in manuscript: 1677. 6¾x4½   Plate VIII.

98 Milford Haven, Victoria, Marchioness of, 1863-   Eldest *daughter of Ludwig IV of Hesse-Darmstadt and Alice, daughter of Queen Victoria. Discontinued foreign title in 1917. Cf. no. 95.*

"VICTORIA"

Armorial lozenge, with the paternal arms of Hesse. Name imposed over the arms, crowned.

Engraving. 3⅛x2¾   Plate XV.

Plate viii

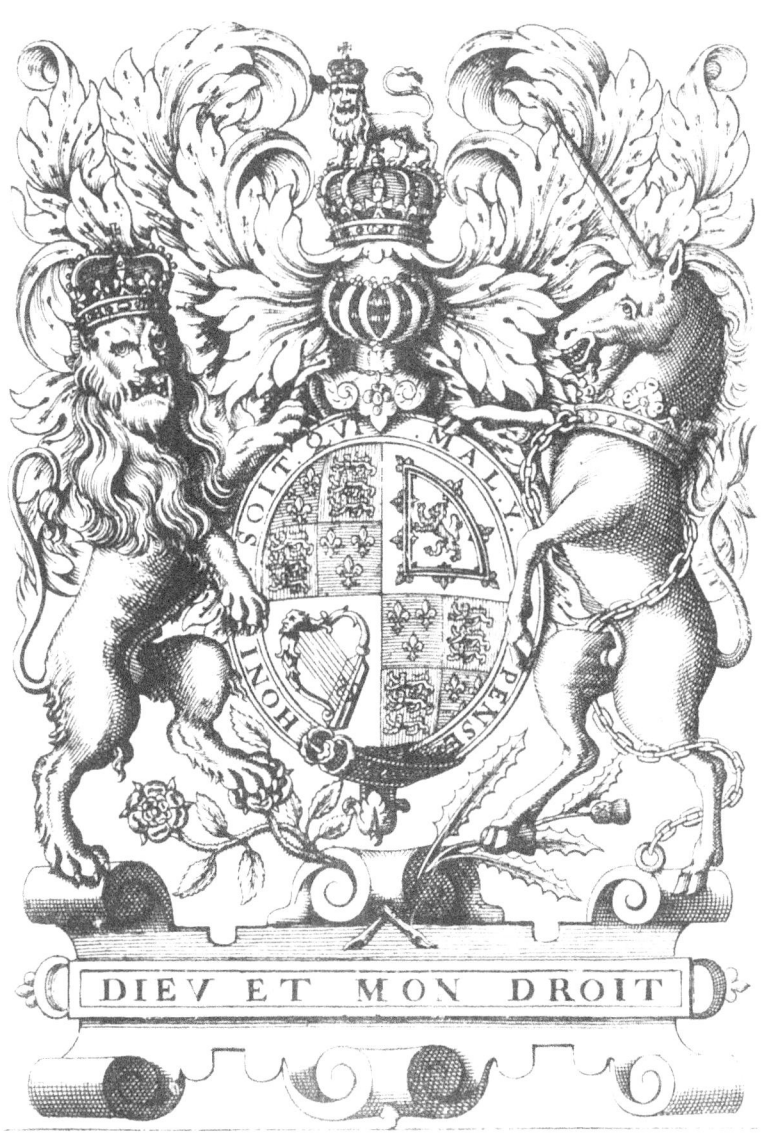

99 **Victoria.**

"VICTORIA"

Label. Name on a ribbon. In appearance like a calling card.

Engraving. 2x3½

Probably not a bookplate.

100 **William, Duke of Gloucester, 1689-1700.** *Son of Queen Anne.*

"DU TRES - HAUT, TRES - PUISSANT, ET TRES - ILLUSTRE PRINCE, GUILLAUME FILS DE LA PRINCESS ANNE, PAR LE PRINCE GEORGE DE DANEMARC; CHEVALIER DU TRES-NOBLE ORDRE DE LA JARTIERE: INSTALLÉ AU CHÂTEAU DE WINDESORE LE 24me. JOUR DE JUILLET, L'AN MDCXCVI."

Early armorial, with supporters and mantling. The royal arms within the Garter, differenced by a label of three points charged with a cross at center, and an escutcheon of pretence charged with the arms of Denmark.

Engraving, signed: I. Sturt Sculp. [1696] 6½x4¼

101 **Frederick Lewis, Prince of Wales, 1707-1751.** *Eldest son of George II.*

"FREDERICK-LEWIS, PRINCE OF WALES, DUKE OF CORN-WALL & EDINBURGH, MARQUESS OF YE ISLE OF ELY, EARL OF CHESTER & ELTHAM, VISCOUNT LAUNCESTON AND BARON OF SNAUDON."

Jacobean armorial, with supporters and mantling. Royal arms, within the Garter, differenced by a label. With the Prince of Wales's motto: Ich dien.

Engraving. 3¾x3½

102 **Fitz George, Thomas Dunckerley.** *Son of George II.*

"THO.ˢ DUNCKERLEY FITZ GEORGE"

Chippendale armorial. The royal arms debruised by a "baton sinister"; motto: Fato non merito. The British lion supported on a cap of maintenance.

Engraving, signed: Levi (I. Levi) Scu. Ports. (Portsea) 1750. 4⅜x3⅛

The identity of sonship, as given in the collection, has not been established by me, though the royal descent is obvious from the arms. C. P.

39

103 Albert, Prince Consort of Queen Victoria, 1819-1861.

"THE PRINCE CONSORT'S MILITARY LIBRARY"

Armorial, with supporters. Arms (1 and 4) of England, differenced by a label of three points, the center point charged with a cross, and (2 and 3) of Saxony; within the Garter. Motto: Treu und Fest. With the rose, thistle, and shamrock, and above, six crests (left to right): Cleve and La Marck, Thüringen, Saxony, Meissen, Jülich, and Berg.

Engraving. 3⅛ x 2⅜

Continental Europe

104 Napoléon I, Emperor of the French, 1769-1821.

"EX LIBRIS N"

Pictorial trophy plate. The French imperial eagle casts a thunder-bolt, which lights up the peaks of the Alps. Below: emblems of war, with an owl, the books of the Napoleonic code, and the cross of the Legion of Honor.

Etching. 4⅞ x 3¾

Napoleon did not use a bookplate. This representation of one, which he might have used, was designed by L. Joly in his *Ex Libris Imaginaires et Supposés de Personnages Célèbres. 1894.*

105 Bonaparte, Louis Lucien, Prince, 1813-1891. *Second son of Lucien, the brother of Napoleon I.*

"EX BIBLIOTHECA LUDOVICI LUCIANI BONAPARTE"

Armorial crest. The Napoleonic eagle surmounted by a princely crown and set within an inscribed oval frame.

Engraving. [ca. 1860] 2⅞ x 2¼   Plate XI.

106 Caroline, Queen of Naples, 1782-1839. *Caroline (Bonaparte Murat), youngest sister of Napoleon I.*

"C"

Armorial. A shield upon a mantle with the letter "C" at center, surrounded by the collar of the Legion of Honor, and surmounted by a prince's crown. The emblems of batons crossed behind the shield and two anchors below indicate a marshal of the Empire and grand marshal respectively.

Engraving. [ca. 1810, reprint 1901] 3½ x 2¾   Plate XII.

A bookplate identical with this "trophy" plate, except that a "J" replaces the "C", exists for Joachim Murat, husband of Caroline, and for whom it seems logical to surmise the design was originally created. The Murat library is now in the Biblioteca Nazionale at Naples, and re-impressions of both bookplates from the copper originals were made in 1901.

107 Napoléon III, Emperor of the French, 1808-1873. *Abdicated 1871.*

"N. BIBLIOTHÈQUE DE S. A. I. MGR. LE PRINCE NAPOLÉON"

Label. The initial "N", with an eagle's head placed at its first bend, is set within an inscribed frame.

Engraving. [ca. 1860] "N" in brown ink. 3x2⅜

108 Victoire, Princess of France, 1733-1799. *Fifth daughter of Louis XV.*

"BIBLIOTHÈQUE DE MADAME VICTOIRE DE FRANCE"

Decorative armorial. The royal arms of France modern on a lozenge. Enclosed in palm sprays tied at the base, where a ribbon slipped through the knot is inscribed with the name. Surmounted by a coronet of rank. The whole within a frame studded with a fleur-de-lis at each corner.

Engraving, signed: C. Baron, Sculp. 3⅛x2⅝

109 Condé, Louise Adélaide de Bourbon, Princesse de, 1757-1824. *Daughter of Louis Joseph de Bourbon, Prince of Condé. Became abbess of Rémiremont, 1786.*

"LOUISE ADELAIDE DE BOURBON"

Armorial lozenge, the royal arms differenced by a "baton peri" of the younger line. Placed within a Jacobean frame, a shell above and resting on a bracket bearing the name, the whole enclosed in palm sprays, and surmounted by a coronet.

Engraving. 3¾x3   Plate II.

110 Louis Philippe, King of France, 1773-1850. *(While Duc d'Orléans).*

[ANONYMOUS]

Armorial. An undecorated center panel is set off by border draperies, while the arms as borne by the King before 1830 are on a small oval shield in an upper compartment—France, differenced by the label of Orléans, with the coronet of princes of the blood. Surrounded by the collars of the Orders of Saint Michel and Saint Esprit, and bordered by royal banners.

Engraving. 5x3¼

111 Munich. Bayerische Staatsbibliothek.

"BIBLIOTHECA REGIA MONACENSIS"

Armorial. The Bavarian arms on a mantle, surmounted by a

Plate ix

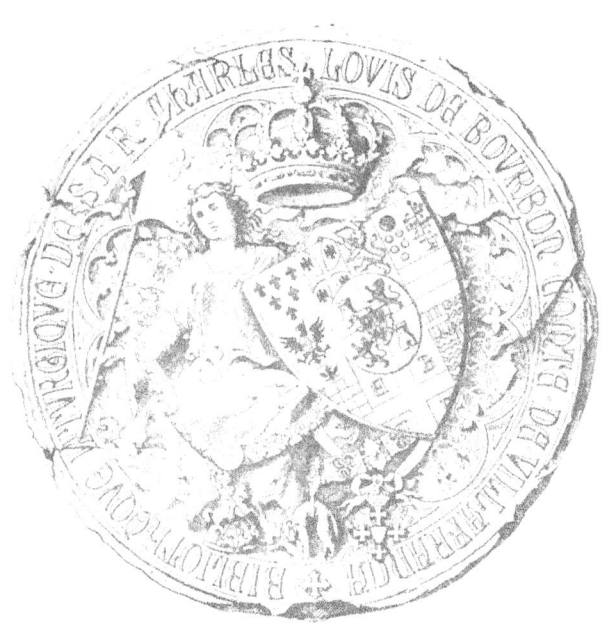

helmet and crown, and supported by lions facing each other. Two royal banners rise from the shield, while collars of three orders are draped below. Beneath all is the inscription, while the whole is enclosed within a double border frame.

Engraving. [ca. 1810] 7x5¼

The founder of the "Königliche, Hof- und Staats-Bibliothek" at Munich was Albert V, Duke of Bavaria, 1550-1579, and bookplates of the library in an infinite number of designs and varieties exist from 1618 on. In the 1850's there was a large sale of duplicates, and the above plate, bearing the stamp "Duplum Bibliothecae R. Monac." might have been removed from a volume disposed of at that time.

112 Charles Louis de Bourbon (Charles II) Duke of Parma, 1799-1883. (While "Conti di Villafranca").

"BIBLIOTHÈQUE LITURGIQUE DE S.A.R. CHARLES LOUIS DE BOURBON, COMTE DE VILLAFRANCA"

Armorial seal. A seated angel, clad in a tunic decorated with fleurs-de-lis, clasps in her right hand a banner charged with the lilies of France, while in her left is supported the shield bearing the arms of Bourbon-Spain and Bourbon-Parma, surmounted by a royal crown. Suspended below are the collars of the Orders of Constantine of Naples (Ordine Constantiniano di San Giorgio), the Golden Fleece, and the cross of the Order of Civil Merit of Lucca. Encircled by the inscription.

Engraving signed: Agry, Gr. [Paris, ca. 1880] Sepia. 5⅜x4¼
Plate IX.

The famous Liturgical collection, for which this plate was designed, was assembled by the Duke after his abdication from Parma in 1849, at which time he assumed the title of Count of Villafranca.

113 Elena, Duchess of Aosta, 1871-   Born "Hélène", Princess of France. Second daughter of Louis Philippe, Comte de Paris.

"HELENAE AUGUSTAE DUCISSAE. EX LIBRIS"

Pictorial armorial, representing a porcupine bearing on its quills a coronet. Border design of fleurs-de-lis.

Etching, signed: ALT.V. Sepia. Proof. 6¼x4¾.   Plate X.

The emblem of a porcupine and crown dates from Louis, Duke of Orleans, brother of Charles VI, who instituted the "Ordre du Porc-Épic" in 1394. It is, however, more popularly associated with his grandson, Louis XII, who used the device in the decorations of the château at Blois, and from whom the Duchess may claim descent from both sides of her family.

43

114 Caroline, Duchess of Berry, 1798-1870. *Eldest daughter of Francesco I, King of the Two Sicilies.*

"BIBLIOTHÈQUE DE ROSNY"

Armorial. Two ovals: dexter, the arms of France differenced by a bordure (the "Duc de Berry" was younger son of Charles X); sinister, arms of the Two Sicilies. Enclosed in lily sprays, interlaced and tied with a cord in lover's knots known as the "lac d'amour." Surmounted by a coronet of rank; below, the inscription.

Engraving. [ca. 1820] 4¼x2½

This plate also exists without the inscription. The library of the Duchess at Rosny (sometimes spelled Resny), Île-de-France, was especially famed for the magnificence of its bindings. A portion of the library was sold in Paris in 1864.

115 Luisa, Infanta of Spain, 1882-   Consort of Carlos, Prince of Bourbon-Sicily, Infante of Spain. *Born "Louise", Princess of France. Youngest daughter of Louis Philippe, Comte de Paris.*

"BIBLIOTECAE LA SERENISIMA SRA INFANTA DONA LUISA. VILLAMANRIQUE"

Decorative armorial. Two ovals accollé, each with the royal arms of France modern, the dexter shield differenced by a bordure. Ensigned with a coronet of rank, and encircled by the inscription. "Villamanrique" (Province of Seville) on a ribbon below. The whole within a frame of a modernized Jacobean style.

Process reproduction. 3½x2

116 Robert de Bourbon (Robert I) Duke of Parma, 1848-1907. *Deposed 1860, when Parma incorporated into the Italian state.*

"BIBLIOTHÈQUE DE S.A.R. MONSEIGNEUR LE DUC DE PARME"

Armorial. Arms, within a Chippendale frame, blazoned as 112 above, and surmounted by a ducal crown. Inscription below.

Engraving, signed: Agry, Paris. [1890] 4¼x3⅛

Robert de Bourbon inherited the Liturgical library of his grandfather, Charles Louis de Bourbon, forming as well an additional collection in history and art in which was inserted this bookplate. The entire collection was sold in Paris, 1932.

117 Bourbon-Busset, Louis Antoine Paul, Vicomte de, 1753-1802.

"BIBLIOTHÈQUE DE LOUIS ANTOINE PAUL BOURBON BUSSET CITOYEN FRANÇAIS. 1793"

Label. Inscription within a leafy border.

Engraving. [1793] 3½x2¼

This plate is usually found pasted over 118, which precedes it in point of time. The two plates graphically illustrate the alteration which took place in aristocratic marks of ownership during the French Revolution.

118 Bourbon-Busset . . .

"BIBLIOTHÈQUE DE M. LE Vte. DE BOURBON BUSSET PREMIER GENTILHOMME DE LA CHAMBRE, EN SURVI-VANCE DE Mgr. COMTE D'ARTOIS COLONEL LIEUTE-NANT COMMANDANT LE RÉGIMENT D'ARTOIS CAVA-LERIE. ELÛ GÉNÉRAL DES ÉTATS DE BOURGOGNE, AN-NÉE 1788"

Armorial, rococo style. Two angels on a billowy cloud support the shield charged with the royal arms differenced by a "baton peri," and with a cross of Jerusalem in the upper part. Surmounted by a coronet.

Engraving, signed: Fme Jourdan sculp. [1788] 3¾x2¼

119 Rothelin, Charles d'Orléans de, 1691-1744. ("Abbé de Bour-bon-Rothelin").

[ANONYMOUS]

Armorial. An oval shield, set within a decorative frame and sur-mounted by a ducal crown, rests upon a base decorated in geometrical patterns typical of the period. An escutcheon of pretence, with the arms of France modern differenced by a "baton peri" and a label, as well as angel supporters, indicate royal descent.

Engraving. 4x3   Plate II.

120 Collège d'Eu. Bibliothèque. Founded in 1729 by Louis Auguste, Duc de Maine (1670-1736). *Legitimized son of Louis XIV and Madame de Montespan.*

"EX LIBER: SER: PRINCIPIS CENOMAN: DUCIS BIBLIOTH: COLL: AUG: FUNDATORIS: 1729"

Armorial trophy plate. The royal arms differenced by a "baton peri" (sinister) and surrounded by the collar of the Order of Saint Esprit. An elaborate design, in which the shield, set against a back-ground of draped flags, rests on a pedestal embellished with a battle scene. A soldier, cannon, and other warlike emblems decorate the foreground.

Engraving. [1729] Proof. 7⅛x5.

"Maine" was derived from the "Cenomanni" of Roman Gaul who earlier occupied the territory, hence the title "Principis Cenoman;" and also Maine being royal domain (1481-1790) it was within the King's right to bestow the titles "Duc de Maine" and "Comte d'Eu" on this favored son. The Jesuit College at Eu was founded by Catherine of Cleves in 1582. The ducal library, therefore, and not the college seems to have been donated by the Duke. Cf. Hamilton. French bookplates, p. 179.

121 Leuchtenberg, Eugène Beauharnais, Duc de, 1781-1824. *Adopted son of Napoléon I.*

"QUEST EDIZIONE APPARTIENE ALLA BIBLIOTECA PARTICOTARE ALLA DI S.A.I. EUGENIO NAPOLEONE DI FRANCIA, VICE-RE D'ITALIA, ARCI-CANCELLIERE DI STATO DELL' IMPERO FRANCESE PRINCIPE DI VENEZIA ECC. ECC. ECC."

Label, with inscription only.

8¼x5

Printed by Giambattista Bodoni at Parma, possibly in 1805, while the Prince was Viceroy of Italy. The simplicity of this book label forms a sharp contrast to the rich bookbindings, stamped with emblems and monograms, for which the library was famous. The library of the Dukes of Leuchtenberg was sold in Zurich and Milan in 1935.

122 Philippe Emmanuel, Duke of Vendôme, 1872-1931. *Born Prince of Bourbon-Orléans. Married Henriette, Princess of Belgium.*

"BIBLIOTHÈQUE DE S.A.R. MONSEIGNEUR LE DUC DE VENDÔME"

Armorial. Arms of France modern, differenced by a label, on an oval shield, surrounded by the Orders of Saint Esprit and the Toison d'Or (Golden Fleece). Set within a modernized Chippendale frame, the princely coronet above; inscription below.

Engraving. [ca. 1920] 2⅜x2⅛   Plate XI.

123 Henriette, Duchess of Vendôme, 1870-   . *Born Princess of Belgium. Granddaughter of Leopold I.*

"BIBLIOTHÈQUE DE S.A.R. MADAME LA DUCHESSE DE VENDÔME PRINCESSE DE BELGIQUE"

Plate X

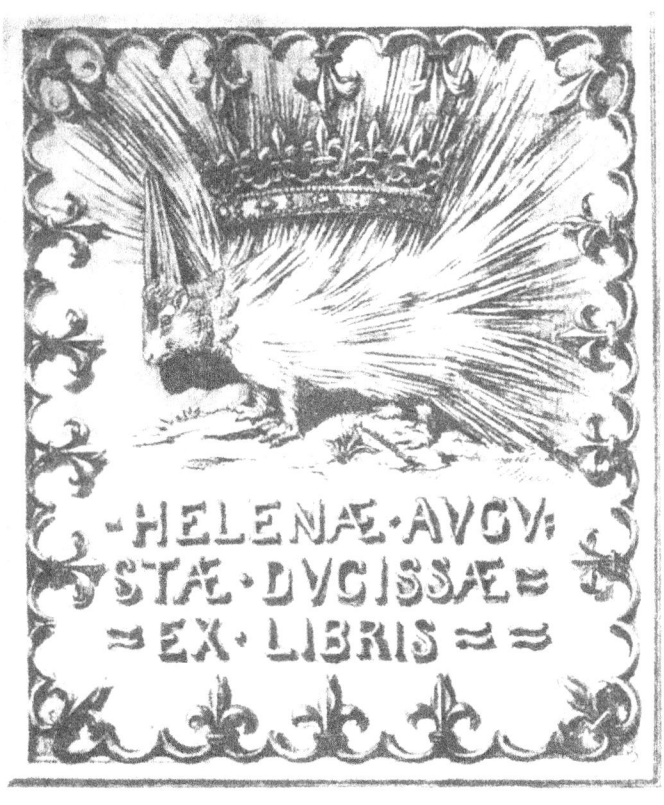

Armorial. Two ovals accollé: dexter, arms of France modern differenced with a label; sinister, the royal lion of Belgium. Enclosed within festoons, and surmounted by the coronet of rank. Inscription below.

Engraving. [ca. 1920] 4½x3¼ Plate XI.

124 Kaiser Wilhelm Dank, Verein der Soldatenfreunde.

"KAISER - WILHELM - DANK, VEREIN DER SOLDATEN-FREUNDE. BEGRÜNDET AM 22 MÄRZ 1897"

Portrait. Before the framed portrait of the Emperor, at the right kneels "Germania" bearing the imperial crown on a cushion, while at the left stands a German knight with the imperial eagle and a sword. In facsimile beneath the picture are the words: "Dem Andenken Kaiser Wilhelm des Grossen. Wilhelm J. R." Indicated below: "Hauptbücherei . . . Nr. . . ."

Process reproduction. [1897] 6x4

125 Kaiser Wilhelm Dank . . .

"KAISER BÜCHEREI DEM KAISER - WILHELM - DANK, VEREIN DER SOLDATENFREUNDE, ZUM 10 JÄHR. REGIERUNGS JUBILÄUM SR. MAJ. KAISER WILHELM II. VON DEUTSCHEN VERLEGERN GESTIFTET"

Portrait. Bust of William II in naval uniform, with facsimile signature below, "Wilhelm J. R." The motto of the Society taken from an utterance of the Kaiser, "Wirke im Andenken an Kaiser Wilhelm den Grossen. Mein Leben und meine Kraft gehören meinen Volke" is at the upper left and right. Inscription below, with indication for "Hauptbücherei Nr. . . ."

Process reproduction. [1907] 6x4

This bookplate, presented by the German publishers at the celebration of the first decade of the Society, superseded the earlier design, no. 124.

126 Kaiser Wilhelm Dank . . .

"ZWEIG - BÜCHEREI DES 'KAISER - WILHELM - DANK, VEREIN DER SOLDATENFREUNDE' FÜR DIE DEUTSCHE BESATZUNG VON KIAUTSCHOU. BEGRÜNDET AM 22 MÄRZ 1898."

Pictorial. The convential German knight with his shield stands at left, while at right is the inscription and indication for "Stamm-Nr. . . ." Below in facsimile German script is the quotation from a speech of William II at Kiel, Dec. 16, 1897: "Möge Jedem, mit dem wir zu thun haben werden, klar sein, dass der deutsche Michel seinen mit dem Reichsadler geschmückten Schild fest auf den Boden gestellt hat, um dem, der ihn um Schutz angeht, ein für allemal diesen Schutz zu gewähren."

Process reproduction. [1898] 6x4

The Germans occupied Tsingtau in 1897.

127   Wilhelm II, King of Württemberg, 1848-1921. *Renounced the throne in 1918 and took at the same time the title of Duke of Württemberg.*

"WILHELM II. PRIVAT-BIBLIOTHEK"

Armorial. Württemberg family arms: three parallel demi-antlers, placed horizontally on a triangular shield; the inscription within the border.

Process reproduction on green parchment. 4⅜x3⅞

128   Hermine, Consort of Wilhelm II, German Emperor, 1887- *Second wife of William II. Born Princess of Reuss, Elder line; married first Prince of Schönaich-Carolath.*

"H"

Pictorial armorial. View of Doorn Castle, Holland. At lower left the crowned cipher "H" within an oval.

Etching. Light blue. 4¾x3¾

129   Augusta Viktoria, Empress Consort of Wilhelm II, German Emperor, 1858-1921. *First wife of William II. Born Princess of Schleswig-Holstein.*

"A V K K EX LIBRIS IMPERATRICIS. NOVI PALATII"

Decorative armorial. A conventionalized design of a square within a square, and a cross upon a cross. Upon the larger square, forming the background, is traced a modified Iron Cross of Prussia. The smaller compartment at center is occupied by two shields, crowned, for Germany and Schleswig-Holstein, and an opened book. Radiating from this, the arms of a slender cross terminate in the letters A V K K (Augusta Viktoria Kaiserin Königin). A ribbon bearing the inscription, "Ex Libris . . ." encircles the center, and ends above with the motto of the Order of the Black Eagle: Suum cuique.

Process reproduction, signed: S (Josef Sattler) [1896] 5x4¼

This bookplate was designed for the volumes in a library built in 1896 at the "New Palace" (erected by Frederick the Great, 1763-1769) near Potsdam.

Plate xi

105

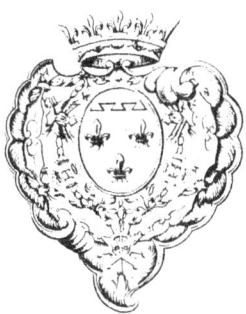

*Bibliothèque de
S.A.R. Monseigneur
le Duc de Vendôme*

122

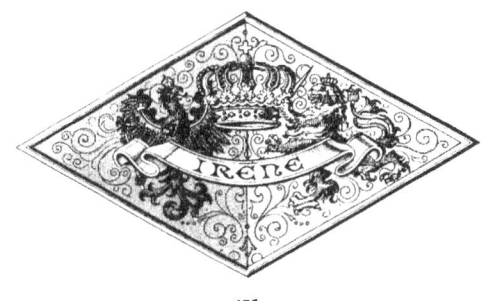

139

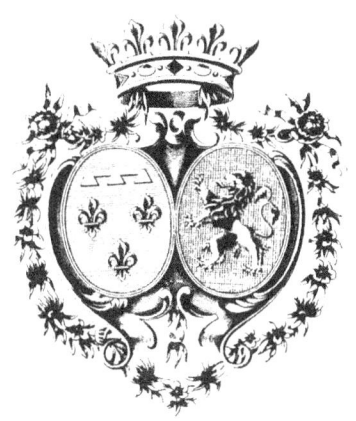

*Bibliothèque de S.A.R.
Madame la Duchesse de Vendôme
Princesse de Belgique*

123

130 Wilhelm, Crown Prince of the German Empire and of Prussia, 1882- *Renounced rights of succession, 1918.*

"WILHELM KRONPRINZ"

Decorative armorial. The Brandenberg family arms, an eagle on a shield, with helmet and lambrequin surmounted by a feathered electoral crown, set within a frame in an early Gothic style of ornamentation. Inscription below.

Process reproduction, signed: G [eorg] Otto, 1903. 4¾x2¾

Copied from a representation of the arms of Otto IV (1266-1309) in the "Manessen Liederhandschrift."

131 Friedrich Franz III, Grand Duke of Mecklenburg-Schwerin, 1851-1897.

"AUS DER BÜCHERSAMMLUNG DES GROSSHERZOGS FRIEDRICH FRANZ VON MECKLENBURG-SCHWERIN"

Pictorial armorial. An elaborate design in Renaissance style of architecture. Within a frame at center is a view of the library interior at Castle Schwerin. Inset within the border frame below is a portrait medallion of the Grand Duke, flanked at either side by figures copied from frescoes of Michel Angelo in the Sistine Chapel at Rome. Above, the Mecklenburg arms, with the House Order and motto: Per aspera ad astra. The inscription at the base.

Photogravure, unsigned. [By Karl Teske and W. Behrens, 1894] Sepia. 6½x4¼

132 Karl Eduard, Duke of Saxe-Coburg and Gotha, 1884- *Born Leopold Charles Edward, 2d Duke of Albany. Became 1900, Duke of Saxe-Coburg and Gotha. Abdicated his right and titles, and removed from the Roll of Peers in Great Britain, 1918.*

"EX LIBRIS CAROLI EDUARDI DUCIS SAXONIAE. PRIVAT BIBLIOTHEK COBURG. 19 . . ."

Armorial. A helmet and lambrequin from which rises the crest, a conical form, charged with the oblique bar of Saxony, and terminating in a tuft of peacock feathers. "Ex libris" and the name encircle the design, while the library designation appears below, followed by "Katalog" and "No."

Process reproduction. 4⅞x3⅜

133 Blücher von Wahlstatt, Gebhard Lebrecht, Fürst, 1865-1931 and Fürstin (Evelyn Mary Stapleton-Bretherton) 1876-

"EX LIBRIS FÜRST UND FÜRSTIN BLÜCHER VON WAHLSTATT"

Pictorial armorial. View of Castle Krieblowitz, home of Prince Blücher, near Breslau, Prussian Silesia. Upper center border, two small ovals accollé (1) for Blücher (two perpendicular keys with notches outward) and (2) Stapleton-Bretherton. Inscription within an escalloped frame below.

Process reproduction, signed: K G H (Karl Gustav von Hiller) 1918. 5¼x3¾

134 Adolf, Prince of Schaumburg-Lippe, 1883-1936.
"ADOLF FUERST ZU SCHAUMBURG-LIPPE"

Armorial. The shield of Schaumburg with the rose of Lippe at center, surmounted by the helmet, mantling and elaborate crest of the ruling prince, or heir apparent, pennons and lances, with plumes of peacock feathers, rising from a coronet.

Process reproduction, signed: O. H. (Otto Hupp) [ca. 1900] 3½x2¾

135 Olga Nikolaevna, Consort of Karl I, King of Württemberg, 1822-1892. *Born Grand Duchess of Russia.*
"O N" (Transliterated from the Russian)

Monogram armorial. A delicately festooned cipher, surmounted by a crown amid rays.

Engraving. [187-] 2⅞x2½

Labouchere incorrectly indicates a monogram of "three" letters, miscalling the Russian "N" (appearing as an ornate "H") the "middle" letter.

136 Ernst Friedrich Carl, Duke of Saxe-Hildburghausen-Altenburg, 1655-1715.
"E F C"

Monogram armorial. A double cipher ensigned with a ruling prince's crown. Enclosed within an oval frame, the border interlaced with ribbons knotted above, while below depend badges of the Orders of the White Falcon (Saxe-Weimar) and Saint Hubert (Bavaria).

Engraving, signed: Martin Tyroff, del. & sc. Norimba. (Nuremberg) [ca. 1714] 5¾x4¼   Plate XIII.

137 Leiningen, Ernst, Fürst von, 1830-1904.
"ARCHIV DES FÜRSTLICHEN HAUSES LEININGEN"

Plate xii

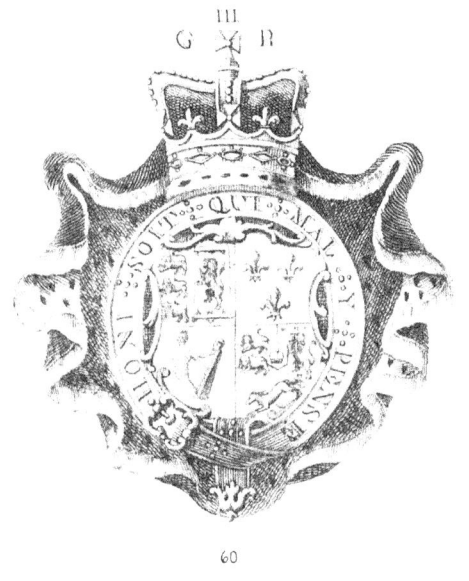

60

G. IV. R.

ROYAL LIBRARY.

66

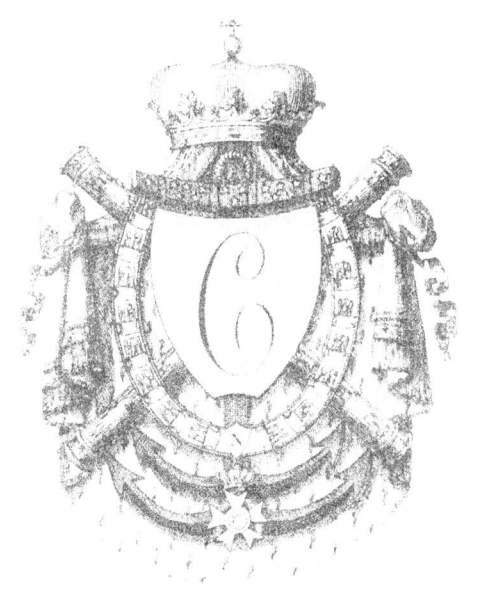

106

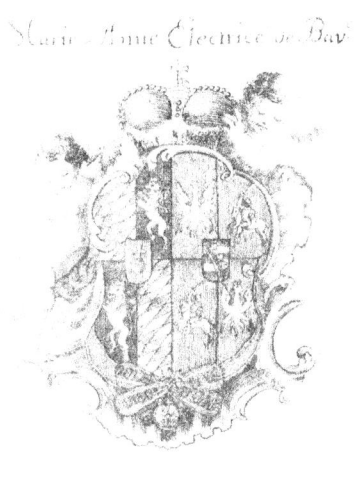

Marie-Anne Électrice de Bav.

148

Armorial. Arms on a shield: three vultures, with a label, crowned. Enclosed within plant sprays, the inscription below.

Wood engraving, signed in monogram: A H (Adolf M. Hildebrandt) 3⅝x3

138 Heinrich, Prince of Prussia, 1862-1929. *Second son of Friedrich III, German Emperor and Victoria, eldest daughter of Queen Victoria. Married Princess Irene, no. 139.*

"PRINZ HEINRICH VON PREUSSEN"

Armorial. The Prussian eagle, sceptre and orb in its claws, the wings overlaid with a clover stem, and on its breast the cipher "F R" (Fridericus Rex). In a Gothic quatrefoil, the name around the border.

Engraving, unsigned. [Designed by Prince Louis of Battenberg, later 1st Marquis of Milford Haven, 1896] 4½x3

139 Irene, Princess Heinrich of Prussia, 1866-　*Born Princess of Hesse-Darmstadt.*

"IRENE"

Armorial. In lozenge form, upon a diapered field, the Prussian eagle and the Hessian lion uphold a royal crown.

Engraving, unsigned. [Designed as no. 138] 3⅛x4½

Plate XI.

140 Waldemar, Prince of Prussia, 1889-　*Eldest son of Prince and Princess Heinrich, nos. 138-39.*

"WALDEMAR"

Armorial. The royal Prussian eagle, surrounded by the collar of the Order of the Black Eagle with the badge suspended beneath. The name on a ribbon. Upon a diamond-shaped ground, with diaper, as no. 139.

Engraving, unsigned. [Probably designed as nos. 138 and 139] 1⅝x2¾

141 Waldemar . . .

"WALDEMAR PRINZ VON PREUSSEN"

Seal armorial. A small oval, with arms as no. 140, encircled by the inscription.

Embossed in red. 1½x1⅛

This "marque of possession" was used to denote ownership of articles of all kinds, not merely books.

142 Umberto, Prince of Piedmont, 1904-   *"Crown Prince,"*
son of Vittorio Emanuele III, King of Italy.

"EX LIBRIS HUMBERTI A SABAVDIA PEDEMONTII PRINCIPIS"

Armorial. The royal arms, the cross of Savoy, differenced by a label, and ensigned with a crown. Surrounded by the collar of the Order of the Annunciation, with the motto of the House of Savoy "Fert," and supported by lions (more recently replaced by the "fasces," badge of the Fascist party). Below, the inscription, enclosed in a compartment bordered with laurel, possibly symbolic of the degree in jurisprudence (the "laurel crown") conferred upon the Prince by the University of Padua in 1923.

Engraving, signed: E. Cotti a Pisa. 3¼ square.

The motto "Fert" is a contraction of "Fortitudo ejus Rhodum tenuit," referring to an expedition of Amedeo V of Savoy (1249-1323)

143 Elena, Queen Consort of Vittorio Emanuele III, King of Italy, 1872-   *Born Princess of Montenegro.*

"EX LIBRIS HELENAE ITALIAE REGINAE"

Armorial. An impaled shield; dexter, the cross of Savoy; sinister, the arms (eagles) of the House of Petrovic Njegos, Montenegro. Supported by kneeling angels, and surmounted by a royal crown. Border decoration of the looped cords of the "lac d'amour." The inscription below on a ribbon.

Etching. Sepia. 4⅞x6

144 Maria Teresa, Queen Consort of Carlo Alberto, King of Sardinia, 1801-1855. *Born "Theresa" of Tuscany, Archduchess of Austria.*

"PROPRIETA DI S. M. LA REGINA MADRE MARIA TERESA 185 . . ."

Label. An oval, lettered in four rows and enclosed in a scroll design.

Lithograph. 185-   1½x2¼

The "Queen Mother" of Vittorio Emanuele II, King of Italy.

145 Borghese, Marco Antonio, Principe di Sulmona, 1814-1886.

"EX LIBRIS M. A. PRINCIPIS BURGHESII"

Armorial seal. Arms of the Borghese, a crowned eagle in the upper division of the shield, a wivern in the lower, on a mantle and surmounted by the crossed keys of Saint Peter and the Papal banner.

The design within a quatrefoil upon an embroidered background, and encircled by the inscription.

Process reproduction from an engraving. [ca. 1860] Sepia. 3¼x2½

The famous Borghese library, founded by Camillo Borghese (Pope Paul V, 1552-1621) was sold in 1892-1893.

146 Charles Louis de Bourbon (Charles II) Duke of Parma, 1799-1883. *(While Duke of Lucca)*

"DI S.A.R. IL DUCA DI LUCCA"

Pictorial armorial. A fluted pedestal, its finial a seated dog, is inscribed "Immota" at its base and "Fides" at top, while at center is borne a crowned shield with the arms of France modern. The legend is lightly engraved at the outer border of the design.

Engraving. [ca. 1830] Light blue. 3¼x2½

147 Maximilian Franz, Elector of Cologne and Bishop of Münster, 1756-1801. *Youngest son of Franz I (German and Roman Empire) and Maria Theresa of Austria.*

"M F"

Monogram armorial. The cipher forms the central theme of the design, while a delicate tracery of branches and leaves from below and rays from an electoral crown above, meet over it.

Etching, signed: Gra. par C. Dupuis, off. (Engraved by Charles Dupuis, Lieutenant of Artillery) [ca. 1785] Light reddish brown. 3¼ square.

148 Maria Anna, Consort of Maximilian Joseph I, Elector of Bavaria, 1728-1797. *Second daughter of Friedrich August II, Elector of Saxony, and King of Poland (as August III, 1733-1763).*

"MARIE ANNE ELECTRICE DE BAV.ᵉ"

Decorative armorial. Arms of Bavaria and Poland-Saxony within an escalloped frame, two cherubs at the sides supporting the Electress's crown above. Surrounded by the ribbon of the Order of Saint Catharine of Russia, with its motto on a knotted ribbon below, transliterated: "Za liubov ī otechestvo" (For love and fatherland).

Engraving. [Cologne, ca. 1770] 4¼x2⅞   Plate XII.

149 Maria de la Paz, 1862-   *Born Infanta of Spain,* and
Ludwig Ferdinand, 1859-   , Princess and Prince of
Bavaria.

"BIBLIOTHEK PAZ UND LUDWIG FERDINAND VON BAYERN"

Armorial. Arms upon two framed ovals, accollé, crowned, for the Prince and Princess; dexter, with an escutcheon of pretence for Bavaria (a field divided by diagonal lines, forming a diamond pattern) and sinister, an inescutcheon for France modern. Draped with collars and badges of the Orders of Saint Hubert and the Golden Fleece.

Process reproduction from an engraving. 4x3

150 Adalbert, Prince of Bavaria, 1886-   *Second son of the Prince and Princess Ludwig Ferdinand, no. 149.*

"EX LIBRIS ADALBERT PRINZ VON BAYERN"

Pictorial, indicating activities and tastes of its owner: a cannon (the Prince was officer of artillery in World War I) and piles of books, suggestive of literary interests and authorship. Above on a ribbon "Ex libris," with a tiny shield bearing the arms of Bavaria at the center of the knot. Below, the name. Sprays of roses decorate the whole.

Etching, signed H. B. (Hugo Bürkner) 5⅜x3½

151 Maria del Pilar, Princess of Bavaria, 1891-   *Only daughter of the Prince and Princess Ludwig Ferdinand, no. 149.*

"EX LIBRIS MARIA DEL PILAR PRINZESSIN V. BAYERN"

Pictorial armorial. A decorative motif with madonna and child, the robe of the madonna extending almost to the lower edge of the plate, the interval beneath being filled with stars, a crescent moon and the name. From the upper portion angel's wings, bordered with roses, radiate outward. A rounded lozenge at lower center bears the paternal arms, while "Ex libris" is at the sides.

Wood engraving, signed in monogram (unidentified) 5⅝x2⅞

152 Ferdinand I, Czar of Bulgaria, 1861-   *Born Duke of Saxe-Coburg and Gotha. Elected King of Bulgaria, 1908; abdicated 1918.*

"EX LIBRIS FERDINANDI I. SAXECOBURGENSIS DUCIS BULGARORUMQUE REGIS AUGUSTI"

Decorative armorial. At center: Arms of Saxe-Coburg-Gotha within a pointed oval in the form of a seal, around its exergue the inscription. Bordered with a conventionalized design and enclosed in a frame, a fleur-de-lis at each corner for maternal descent from the House of Orléans.

Process reproduction from an engraving, signed: Hirsch, Sc. Paris, A de F del. 4⅞x4⅛

Plate xiii

153   Boris III, Czar of Bulgaria, 1894-1943.

"ĪZ KNĪGĪTIE NA BORIS III TSAR' NA B"LGARĪTIE" (Transliterated from the Bulgarian) Translated: From the books of Boris III, Czar of Bulgaria.

Decorative armorial. At center, arms of Bulgaria (a crowned lion) surmounted by a royal crown, and encircled by the collar of the Order of Saint Cyril and Saint Method (instituted by Ferdinand I in 1909), with badge beneath. Surrounded by a garter bearing the inscription; the whole enclosed in a frame with border decoration.

Process reproduction. 5x4⅛

154   Marie Louise, Queen Consort of Ferdinand I, Czar of Bulgaria, 1870-1899. *Born Princess of Bourbon-Parma.*

"MARIE LOUISE. EX LIBRIS"

Pictorial. A delicate framework, rising from a Chippendale base inscribed "Ex libris," supports a centre tablet above with the name. Ornamented with festoons and rose clusters.

Engraving, unsigned. [By George W. Eve, ca. 1914] 4x2¾ Eve no. 255.   Plate IV.

155   Manuel II, King of Portugal, 1889-1932. *Deposed 1910.*

"EX LIBRIS. DEPOIS DE VÓS NÓS D. MANUEL II"

Pictorial armorial. Two main compartments: dexter, the arms of Portugal, five shields charged with bezants and a bordure charged with seven castles, crowned; sinister, the armillary sphere, originally the device of Manuel I (1469-1521) which, with the rope border enclosing the design, is symbolic of the maritime greatness of the Portuguese nation in the 15th and 16th centuries. "Ex libris" above, with the remainder of the inscription below.

Wood engraving. 3⅞x3

156   Lubomirski, Jerzy, Książę, 1882-   *Prince of the Polish nobility.*

"EX LIBRIS GEORGII LUBOMIRSKI"

Armorial. Arms: a wavy band crosses the shield. With supporters (lions), and surmounted by a princely coronet. Enclosed within a garter bearing the inscription.

Engraving, signed: R. O. 1929, J. & E.B. 6⅛x4¼

157 Oscar II, King of Sweden, 1829-1907.

"O II"

Pictorial armorial. The "II" set within an "O", framed in laurel sprays tied at the base with a ribbon, and surmounted by a royal crown. A motto below reads, "Öfver djupen mot höjden" (Beyond the depths, towards the height)

Wood engraving, unsigned. [By Agi Lindegren, 1895] 3⅛x2½

A design receiving the award at a prize competition instituted to provide a bookplate for His Majesty's library. The motto is quoted from a travel sketch, written by the King.

158 Unidentified Russian prince.

"EX LIBRIS. U O Ï" (Transliterated from the Russian)

Pictorial. A Greek temple crowns a slope above the sea. In the upper border is inscribed "Ex libris," flanked by the motto, "Se inserit astris," while in the foreground below a male and a female figure, each in Grecian costume hold suspended between them a rope of laurel above the letters "Y O Ï."

Engraving. Proof. 10x7.

Caption as indicated in the Collection.

159 Mikhaïl Mikhaïlovich, Grand Duke of Russia, 1861-1929. *Grandson of Nicholas I. Married morganatically Sophy, Countess of Torby, no. 161.*

"M M. EX LIBRIS. GRAND DUKE MICHAEL OF RUSSIA"

Monogram armorial. A decorative cipher of two Ms crossed, and ensigned by an imperial crown. "Ex libris" is inscribed within the upper border, while the name is enclosed in a lower compartment beneath the monogram.

Engraving. Proof. 10x7.

160 Mikhaïl Mikhaïlovich . . .

"M M. EX LIBRIS. GRAND DUKE MICHAEL OF RUSSIA"

Design as above.

Engraving. 3⅝x2⅞   Plate XV.

161 Torby, Sofiia Nikolaevna, Grafinia, 1868-   *Born Countess of Merenberg. Daughter of Nikolaus, Prince of Nassau, by his morganatic wife, Natalie Alexandrovna (Pushkïn),*

Plate xiv

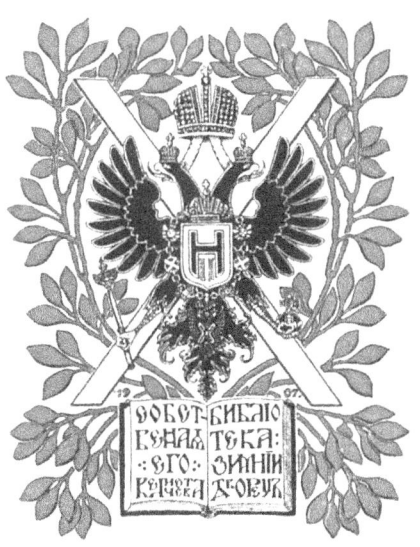

Countess of Merenberg. Morganatic wife of Prince Michael, no. 159.

"S de T"

Pictorial. Landscape, showing elephants and palm trees in an African setting, with a border decoration of entwined snakes. Motto below, "Cette animal est fort méchant quand on l'attaque, il se défends." Above, the monogram, ensigned with the coronet of a countess.

Engraving. 4⅜x3½

While an explanation for the above plate was not located, reference was found to the Countess's penchant for elephants. The Villa Kasbek at San Remo was said to be "full of them, great and small, in china, wood, bronze and every conceivable material."

162 Alexandra, Empress Consort of Nicholas II, Emperor of Russia, 1872-1918. *Born Princess of Hesse-Darmstadt; granddaughter of Queen Victoria.*

"FEODOROVNA"

Pictorial armorial. Three cherubs bear a wavy ribbon with the motto, "Naught but the highest shall content my soul" enclosed in sprays of roses and lilies. Above, on a cartouche a crowned cipher "A F" and below on a ribbon "Feodorovna".

Engraving, signed: W P B (Barrett) 1904. 3⅞x2¾

163 Mariia, Grand Duchess of Russia, 1890-   *Daughter of Grand Duke Paul Alexandrovich and Alexandra Georgievna, Princess of Greece.*

"ĪZ KNĪG EIA IMPERATORSKAGO VYSOCHESTVA VEL Ī-KOĬ KNIAGĪNĪ MARIĬ PAVLOVNY" (Transliterated from the Russian) Translated: From the books of her Imperial Highness, the Grand Duchess Maria Pavlovna.

Decorative armorial. A highly ornamented frame of lattice and scroll work, roses, and cornucopias encloses a center compartment with the inscription. Above this, on a mantle, a small lozenge, with supporters, bears the Russian imperial eagle, crowned, which is in turn surmounted by a rayed crown. In a small compartment below is the crowned monogram "M P", with the ribbon and badge of the Order of Saint Catherine of Russia.

Process reproduction, signed: B.Z. 4¾x3¾

164 Alexander II, Emperor of Russia, 1818-1881.

"A N" (Transliterated from the Russian, i.e. Aleksandr Nīkolaevīch)

Monogram armorial. The cipher is placed "in the clouds" and ensigned with an imperial crown adorned with rays.

Reproduced from an engraving. $2\frac{5}{8}$x$2\frac{1}{4}$

165 Alexander III, Emperor of Russia, 1845-1894.

"A A" (Aleksandr Aleksandrovĭch)

Monogram armorial. The cipher within a cloud, surmounted by a rayed crown, similar to no. 164.

Engraving. [ca. 1856] $2\frac{3}{4}$x$2\frac{7}{8}$

Vereshchagin attributes ownership to Alexander II (1818-1881) who was, however, the son of Nicholas I, or, Aleksandr Nĭkolaevĭch.

166 Sergeĭ Aleksandrovĭch, Grand Duke of Russia, 1857-1905. *Fourth son of Alexander II.*

"S A" (Transliterated from the Russian)

Monogram armorial. A graceful cipher (as "C A" in the Russian) on a cartouche, within a border frame of roses and leafy sprays, surmounted by a crown.

Engraving. 5x4

167 Petr Nĭkolaevĭch, Grand Duke of Russia, 1864-1931. *Grandson of Nicholas I.*

"P N" (Transliterated from the Russian)

Monogram armorial. Cipher, surmounted by a crown. "No. 667" printed below.

Process reproduction. 2x$1\frac{1}{2}$

This plate was used exclusively for journals.

168 Belosel'skĭĭ-Belozerskĭĭ, Aleksandr Mikhaĭlovĭch, Kniaz', 1752-1809. *Prince of the Russian nobility.*

"BIBLIOTHÈQUE DU PRINCE BELOSSELSKY DE BELOZERSK"

Armorial. Arms: Two fish swimming crosswise in a river, above them a Greek cross over a crescent. Within a garter bearing the motto: Cor unum via una. Surmounted by a crown. Inscription below.

Engraving. $4\frac{3}{8}$x3

Plate xv

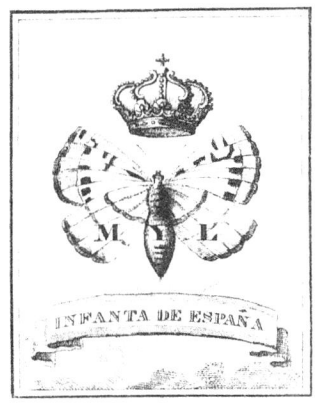

174

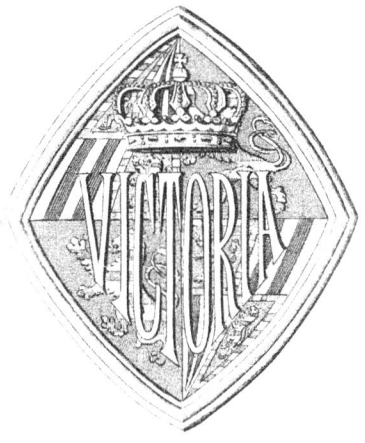

98

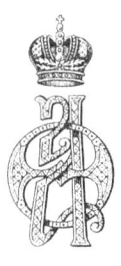

170

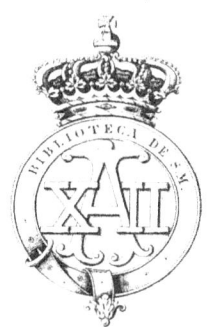

175

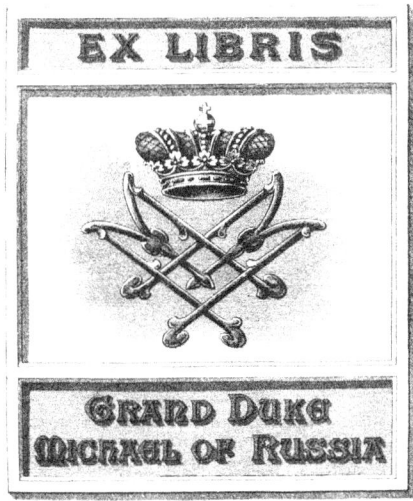

160

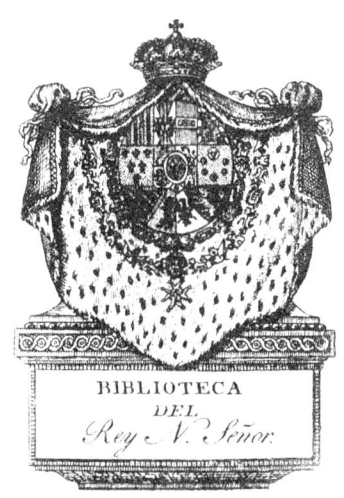

172

169 Nicholas II, Emperor of Russia, 1868-1918.

"N II. SOBSTVENNAIA EGO VELICHESTVA BIBLIOTEKA. ZIMNIĬ DVORETS" (Transliterated from the Russian) Translated: N II. His Majesty's library. Winter Palace.

Decorative armorial. The black double-headed eagle of imperial Russia, crowned with the distinctive crown of "Holy Russia"; on its breast a shield, with the cipher "N II", which is encircled with the collar of the Order of Saint Andrew, the pendant badge upon the eagle's tail. In the dexter claw is held the sceptre, and in the sinister the orb. Placed upon a cross of Saint Andrew (blue), with the inscription on an opened book below. The whole framed within sprays of golden-leaved laurel.

Process reproduction in black, blue and gold. 1907. 3⅛x2⅜

Plate XIV.

170 Alexandra, Empress Consort of Nicholas II, Emperor of Russia, 1872-1918.

"A F" (Transliterated from the Russian, i.e. Alexandra Feodorovna).

Monogram armorial. The delicate "jewel" plate of the Czarina, the monogram ensigned with an imperial Russian crown.

Engraving, unsigned. [Designed by A. E. Fel'kerzam, 1914] Diamond-shaped: 2⅛x2½ across the corners.   Plate V.

171 Alekseĭ Nĭkolaevĭch, Cesarevitch of Russia, 1904-1918.

"ĬZ BĬBLIOTEKA E.I.V. NASLIEDNĬKA TSESAREVĬCHA I VEL. K. ALEKSIEIA NĬKOLAEVĬCHA" (Transliterated from the Russian) Translated: From the library of His Imperial Highness, heir to the throne, Cesarevitch and Grand Duke Alexis Nĭkolaevĭch.

Pictorial armorial. The figure of a "dark angel" (silver gray) with golden wings bears a shield charged with the imperial Russian eagle (black on gold), upon which is superimposed the cipher "N II". Rays and the inscription encircle the head of the angel.

Process reproduction in black, silver, and gold, unsigned. [Designed by A. E. Fel'kerzam, 1907] 4¼x2¾

172 Fernando VII, King of Spain, 1784-1833.

"BIBLIOTECA DEL REY N. SEÑOR"

Armorial. An oval shield with the arms of Spain upon an ermine mantle, surrounded by the collars of the Orders of the Golden Fleece and Carlos III, and ensigned with a crown. Placed upon an architectural bracket, in the style of the First Empire, enclosing space for the inscription at its base.

Engraving. 3⅛x2¼   Plate XV.

Vindel dates this bookplate second half of the 18th century, and states it was used by Carlos III and Carlos IV (ruling 1759-1808). Another impression exists with a slight variation in the form of the lettering.

173 Fernando VII . . .

"BIBLIOTECA DEL REY N. SEÑOR"

Design as above.

Engraving. In carmine. 4⅞x3¼

174 Isabel II, Queen of Spain, 1830-1904. *(While Infanta of Spain) Abdicated 1870.*

"M Y L" (Maria Ysabel Luisa) "INFANTA DE ESPAÑA"

Pictorial armorial. A butterfly with the initials "M," "Y" and "L" on its spread wings and body. Above, a crown, and below on a ribbon: Infanta de España.

Engraving. 3⅛x2⅜   Plate XV

Attributed by Vindel to Maria Luisa (Fernanda) 1832-1897, sister of "Ysabel".

175 Alfonso XII, King of Spain, 1857-1885.

"BIBLIOTECA DE S.M. A XII"

Monogram armorial. "A" with "XII" superimposed, surrounded by a garter bearing the inscription, and ensigned by a royal crown.

Engraving. [ca. 1880] Carmine. 3⅜x3¼   Plate XV.

176 Maria Cristina, Queen Consort of Alfonso XII, King of Spain, 1858-1929. *Born Archduchess of Austria.*

"M. C. R.ª de E.ª" (Maria Cristina, Reina de España)

Decorative armorial. The letters "M." and "C." framed within two floral wreaths placed side by side. "R.ª de E.ª" beneath, with a single fleur-de-lis below. Surmounted by a rayed crown.

Engraving. [19—] 2½x1¾

177 Alfonso XIII, King of Spain, 1886-1941. *Left Spain when the Republic proclaimed, 1931.*

"EX LIBRIS. YLDEPHONSI. XIII. A. NATIVITATE. HIS-
PANIARUM. REGIS"

Armorial. A tiny representation on an oval of the national arms as
borne by the former monarch of Spain, with quarterings for Aragon,
Sicily, Austria, Burgundy, Tuscany, Flanders, Brabant, etc., and on
a circle at center France modern "in pretence" for Bourbon. Ensigned with a crown, and surrounded by the collar of the Order of
the Golden Fleece, with the badge suspended, as well as a second
badge, probably that of the Order of Military Merit of Spain.

Process reproduction in color. 2⅞x2¼

178 Maximilian I, Emperor of Mexico, 1832-1867. *Born Archduke of Austria.*

"M M I"

Armorial. Arms of Mexico (the Mexican eagle holding in its beak
the serpent of Aztec legend) within an oval, supported by gryphons
and surrounded by the collar of an Order (indistinguishable) with
the motto on a ribbon beneath: Equidad en la justicia. Ensigned
with a crown, while below all is placed the cipher.

Engraving. [ca. 1866] 2⅜x2⅜

After his execution, the library of the Emperor was carried from
Mexico to Leipzig and sold. Volumes purchased from the collection,
and containing the bookplate, are to be found in the Bancroft Library
of the University of California.

179 Kalakaua, King of Hawaii, 1836-1891. *Acceded 1874.*

[ANONYMOUS]

Seal armorial. A tiny seal, bearing the Hawaiian arms, ensigned with
a crown and supported by two "kahili" bearers. Below, on a ribbon:
Na mau ke ea o ka aina i ka pono (The life of the land is established
in righteousness)

Embossed in blue. 2½x2¼

The quotation, taken from a speech of King Kamehameha III, July
31, 1843, was adopted as the motto of the Hawaiian Kingdom.

180 Lascaris, Eugene (Prince of Greece).

"EK.TŌN.BIBLIŌN.TOU.BASILIKOU . KAI.AUTOKRATORI-
KOU.OIKOU.TŌN.LASKAREŌN." (From the books of the royal
and imperial house of Lascaris)

Decorative armorial. Arms on a medallion: the double-headed
eagle, with both heads crowned, of the imperial line of Lascaris.

Above, an eastern crown inset with precious stones and tiny pictures, all in color, and the motto of the House, "Meta skotos elpizo fos" (In darkness I hope for light). A red ribbon behind the medallion is drawn together below it with a tassel of coins, while the inscription describes a half-circle at the base.

Process reproduction in colors. [ca. 1930] 6x3

Prince Eugene is the descendant of a noble Byzantine family living in retirement at Saragossa, Spain. Legitimate representative of the dynasty of Morea in southern Greece, he had a following as the logical candidate for the throne of that country before the return of the Danish line to the Greek throne in 1935. Not in the *Almanach de Gotha.*

181 Ashurbanipal, King of Assyria, fl. B.C. 650.

A transcription in cuneiform characters of the formula used by King Ashurbanipal as a "mark of possession." With accompanying translation (given here only in part): "The palace of Ashur-bani-pal, King of hosts, King of Assyria, who putteth his trust in the gods Ashur and Bêlit, on whom Nabû and Tashmêtu have bestowed ears which hear and eyes which see . . . Whosoever shall carry off this tablet, or shall inscribe his name upon it side by side with mine own, may Ashur and Bêlit overthrow him in wrath and anger, and may they destroy his name and posterity in the land."

7⅜x4⅞

The earliest known record of an "Ex libris" (and a royal one). Deciphered from clay tablets excavated from the Royal library at ancient Ninevah and now in the British Museum.

A Selected Bibliography

HERALDRY AND GENEALOGY

Allstrom, C. M. *Dictionary of Royal Lineage.* Chicago, 1902. 2 v.

Almanach de Gotha; Annuaire Généalogique, Diplomatique et Statistique. Gotha, 1941, and earlier vols.

Boutell, Charles. *Boutell's Manual of Heraldry* . . . rev. ed. . . . London, F. Warne, 1931. 332 p. illus., plates.

Boutell, Charles. *Handbook to English Heraldry.* 11th ed., rev. . . . London, 1914. 351 p. illus.

Burke, Sir. J. B. *Genealogical and Heraldic History of the Peerage and Baronetage.* 93rd ed. London, 1935, and earlier editions. illus.

Cokayne, G. E. *The Complete Peerage. v. 13. Peerage Creations. 1901-1938.* London, 1940. 630 p.

Davenport, Cyril. *English Heraldic Book-Stamps.* London, 1909. 450 p. illus.

Doyle, J. W. E. *The Official Baronage of England* . . . 1066–1885. London, 1886. 3 v. illus.

Fairbairn, James. *Fairbairn's Crests of the Leading Families in Great Britain and Ireland.* New York, 1911. 613 p. plates.

Guigard, Joannis. *Armorial du Bibliophile.* Paris, 1870-73. 2 v. in 1. illus.

Muquardt, Charles. *Das Buch der Ritterorden und Ehrenzeichen.* Brussel, 1856. 422 p. col. plates.

Ruvigny, M. H. (de Massue) 9th Marquis of Ruvigny. *The Titled Nobility of Europe.* 1914. 1594 p. illus.

Ströhl, H. G. *Deutsche Wappenrollen.* Stuttgart, 1897. 98 p. illus., col. plates.

BOOKPLATES

Ex Libris, Buchkunst und Angewandte Graphik (Deutscher Verein für Exlibriskunst und Gebrauchsgraphik) Jahr. 1-47. Berlin, 1891-1939. illus., plates.

Ex Libris Society, London. *Journal.* v. 1-18. London, 1892-1909. illus., plates.

Revista Ibérica de Ex Libris. v. 1-4. Barcelona, 1903-06. illus., plates.

Andrews, Irene D. *Owners of Books*. Washington, 1936. 271 p. illus.

Barnett, P. N. *Armorial book-plates*. Sydney, 1932. 172 p. illus.

Dodgson, Campbell, "The New Windsor Castle Bookplates by Stephen Gooden," *in* Fowler, Alfred, ed. *The Romance of Fine Prints*. Kansas City, 1938. p. 59-60.

Gelli, Jacopo. *3500 Ex Libris Italiani*. Milano, 1908. 535 p. plates.

Hamilton, Walter. *Dated Book-Plates*. London, 1895. 225 p. illus.

Hamilton, Walter. *French Book-Plates*. London, 1896. 360 p. illus.

Krieger, Bogdan. "Die Hohenzollern und ihre Bücher," *in Hohenzollern Jahrbuch, 1903*. Berlin [1903] p. 112-141.

Labouchere, Norna. *Ladies' Book-Plates*. London, 1895. 358 p. illus., plates.

Leiningen-Westerburg, K. E. *German Book-Plates*. London, 1901. 531 p. illus.

Vindel, Francisco. *Catalogo Descriptivo de Ex Libris Hispano-Americanos (1588-1900)*. Madrid, 1929. 144 p. plates.

Warnecke, Friedrich. *Die Deutschen Bücherzeichen (Ex-Libris)* Berlin, 1890. 255 p. plates.

––––––––––

Sherborn, C. D. *A Sketch of the Life and Work of Charles William Sherborn, with a Catalogue of his Bookplates*. London, 1912. 109 p. plates.

Viner, G. H. *A Descriptive Catalogue of the Bookplates Designed and Etched by George W. Eve*. Kansas City, 1916. 93 p. plates.

––––––––––

The great foreign encyclopedias should be mentioned as valuable sources of information: *Enciclopedia Italiana di Scienze, Lettere ed Arti*. Rome, 1929-39. 36 v.; *Enciclopedia Universal Ilustrada,* published by Espasa, Barcelona, 1908-30. 72 v.; *La Grande Enclopédie*. Paris, 1886-1902. 31 v. The list of royal bookplates from the Catalogue of the Franks bequest to the British Museum, and the sales catalogues of Gerald Massey of London are useful for checking.

Index

Arabic numerals refer to the numbers in the catalogue; plates are in Roman characters. Monograms are listed under the first letter of the monogram only. A given name without country designation in a main entry (not a cross-reference) implies Great Britain.

Athlone, Countess of. *See* Alice

Augusta Viktoria, Empress Consort of Wilhelm II, German Emperor, 129

Augustus Frederick, Duke of Sussex, 68-69, 71

AUSTRIA, Archduke of. *See* Maximilian Franz, Elector of Cologne
See also Maximilian I ("Ferdinand"), Emperor of Mexico; Arch-
duchesses of: Maria Cristina, Queen Consort of Alfonso XII of Spain;
Maria Teresa (Tuscany), Queen Consort of Carlo Alberto of Sardinia.

Battenberg (Since 1917 Mountbatten), Prince of. *See* Henry, Prince of
Battenberg; Princess of: Beatrice, Princess Henry
See also Carisbrooke, Milford Haven

Bavaria, Electress of. *See* Maria Anna, Consort of Maximilian Joseph I;
Princes of: Adalbert, Ludwig Ferdinand (*under* Maria de la Paz);
Princesses of: Maria de la Paz, Maria del Pilar

Beatrice, Princess Henry of Battenberg, 51, IV

Beauharnais, Eugène de. *See* Leuchtenberg

BELGIUM, Princess of. *See* Henriette, Duchess of Vendôme

Belosel'skii-Belozerskii, Aleksandr Mikhaĭlovĭch, Kniaz', 168

Berry, Duchess of. *See* Caroline, Duchess of Berry

Biblioteca del Rey N. Señor. *See* Fernando VII

Bibliotheca Regia Monacensis. *See* Munich. Bayerische Staatsbibliothek

Blücher von Wahlstatt, Gebhard Lebrecht, Fürst and Fürstin, 133

Bonaparte, Caroline. *See* Caroline, Queen of Naples

—Louis Lucien, Prince, 105, XI

—Napoléon. *See* Napoléon I, Napoléon III

Borghese, Marco Antonio, Principe di Sulmona, 145

Boris III, Czar of Bulgaria, 153

Bourbon, Charles Louis de. *See* Charles Louis de Bourbon

—Louise Adélaide de. *See* Condé

—Robert de. *See* Robert de Bourbon

Bourbon-Busset, Louis Antoine Paul, Vicomte de, 117-118

Bourbon-Condé, Princess of. *See* Condé

Bourbon-Orléans, Prince of. *See* Philippe Emmanuel, Duke of Vendôme;
Princesses of: Elena, Duchess of Aosta; Luisa (Princess Carlos of
Bourbon-Sicily), Infanta of Spain

Bourbon-Parma, Princess of. *See* Marie Louise, Queen Consort of Ferdinand I of Bulgaria

Bourbon-Rothelin. *See* Rothelin

Bourbon-Sicily, Princesses of. *See* Caroline, Duchess of Berry; Luisa (Princess Carlos of Bourbon-Sicily), Infanta of Spain

BULGARIA. (Chronologically arranged) *See* Ferdinand I; Maria Louise, Queen Consort of Ferdinand I; Boris III

Burghese. *See* Borghese

Busset. *See* Bourbon-Busset

C. *See* Caroline, Queen of Naples

C A. (Russian). *See* Sergei Aleksandrovīch

Cambridge, 2d Duke of. *See* George, 2d Duke of Cambridge

Cambridge (Previous to 1917 Teck). *See* Teck

Cambridge. University. Library, 3, II; 4-7

Carisbrooke, Alexander Albert Mountbatten, 1st Marquis of, 53

Caroline, Duchess of Berry, 114

Caroline, Queen of Naples, 106, XII

Cenoman, Prince of. *See* Collège d'Eu. Bibliothèque

Charles I, 30

Charles II, 97, VIII

Charles Edward, Duke of Saxe-Coburg and Gotha. *See* Karl Eduard

Charles Louis de Bourbon, Duke of Parma, 112, IX; 146

Charlotte, Queen Consort of George III, 61-62

Collège d'Eu. Bibliothèque, 120

Cologne, Elector of. *See* Maximilian Franz

Condé, Louise Adélaide de Bourbon, Princesse de, 109, II

Connaught, Duchess of. *See* Louisa Margaret

Cornwall, Duchy of, 76, V

DENMARK, Princess of. *See* Alexandra, Queen Consort of Edward VII

E. *See* Edward, Duke of Windsor

E VII. *See* Edward VII

E F C. *See* Ernst Friedrich Carl

E R. Royal Library, Windsor Castle. *See* Windsor Castle

Edward VII, 86, VII; 87, VI
　　See also Windsor Castle

Edward VIII. *See* Edward, Duke of Windsor

Edward, Duke of Windsor, 29, 89

George V, 22; 88, VI
See also George V and Queen Mary; Royal Body Guard of the King; Windsor Castle

George V and Queen Mary, 24-28

George VI, 36
See also Windsor Castle

George, Prince of Cambridge. See George, 2d Duke of Cambridge

George, 2d Duke of Cambridge, 75

George Frederick Ernest Albert, Prince of Wales. See George V

GERMANY. (Sovereigns chronologically) See Victoria, Empress Consort of Friedrich III; Augusta Viktoria, Empress Consort of Wilhelm II; Hermine, Consort of Wilhelm II. Princes of: Wilhelm, Crown Prince; Heinrich; Waldemar. Princess of: Irene
See also Louisa Margaret, Duchess of Connaught

Gloucester, Dukes of. See Henry, William, William Frederick

GREAT BRITAIN AND IRELAND. (Sovereigns chronologically) See Henry VIII and Katharine of Aragon; Elizabeth; James I; Charles I; Charles II; George III; Charlotte, Queen Consort of George III; George IV; William IV; Victoria; Albert, Prince Consort of Queen Victoria; Edward VII; Alexandra, Queen Consort of Edward VII; George V; Mary, Queen Consort of George V; Edward, Duke of Windsor (Edward VIII); George VI; Elizabeth, Queen Consort of George VI
See also Windsor Castle. Royal Library

—Princes of. See Augustus Frederick, Duke of Sussex; Frederick, Duke of York and Albany; Frederick Lewis, Prince of Wales; George, 2d Duke of Cambridge; Henry, Duke of Gloucester; Leopold, Duke of Albany; William, Duke of Gloucester; William Frederick, 2d Duke of Gloucester and Edinburgh
See also Karl Eduard, Duke of Saxe-Coburg and Gotha

—Princesses of. See Alice, Countess of Athlone; Beatrice, Princess Henry of Battenberg; Helena, Princess Christian of Schleswig-Holstein; Helena Victoria, Princess of Schleswig-Holstein; Louisa Margaret, Duchess of Connaught; Louise, Duchess of Fife; Mary, Countess of Harewood; Mary Adelaide, Duchess of Teck; Sophia; Victoria (dau. of Edward VII)
See also Elizabeth, Consort of Friedrich VI, Landgrave of Hesse-Homburg; Maud, Queen Consort of Haakon VII of Norway; Victoria, Empress Consort of Friedrich III of Germany

Guillaume, fils de la Princess Anne. See William, Duke of Gloucester

H. See Hermine

H-Gloucester. See Henry, Duke of Gloucester

Parma, Dukes of. *See* Charles Louis de Bourbon; Robert de Bourbon

Paz. *See* Maria de la Paz

Petr Nīkolaevīch, Grand Duke of Russia, 167

Philippe Emmanuel, Duke of Vendôme, 122, XI

Piedmont, Prince of. *See* Umberto

Pilar. *See* Maria del Pilar

PORTUGAL, King of. *See* Manuel II

Prince Consort's Military Library. *See* Albert

Prince of Wales and the Bishop of Osnaburgh. *See* George IV and Frederick, Duke of York and Albany

Prince of Wales's Library. *See* George IV

Prussia. *See* Germany

The Queen to Her Army. *See* Victoria, Queen

R A G. *See* George II

R I 6. *See* James I

Resny. *See* Rosny

Reuss, Princess of. *See* Hermine, Consort of Wilhelm II of Germany

Rosny, Bibliothèque de. *See* Caroline, Duchess of Berry

Rothelin, Charles d'Orléans de ("Abbé de Bourbon-Rothelin"), 119, II

Royal Body Guard of the King "G v R", St. James's Palace, 1

Royal Library, Windsor Castle. *See* Windsor Castle

RUSSIA. (Sovereigns chronologically) *See* Alexander III, Nicholas II, Alexandra, Empress Consort of Nicholas II; Grand Dukes of: Alekseĭ Nīkolaevīch (Cesarevitch), Mīkhaĭl Mīkhaĭlovīch, Petr Nīkolaevīch, Sergeĭ Aleksandrovīch; Grand Duchess of: Mariia
See also Olga Nikolaevna, Consort of Karl I, King of Württemberg

S. *See* Charlotte

S A. *See* Sergeĭ Aleksandrovīch

S de T. *See* Torby, Sofiia de

Sardinia, Queen of. *See* Maria Teresa, Consort of Carlo Alberto

Savoy. *See* Italy

Saxe-Coburg and Gotha, Duke of. *See* Karl Eduard
See also Albert, Prince Consort of Queen Victoria; Ferdinand I, Czar of Bulgaria

Saxe-Hilburghausen-Altenburg, Duke of. *See* Ernst Friedrich Carl

Saxony, Princess of. *See* Maria Anna, Consort of Maximilian Joseph I of Bavaria

Schaumburg-Lippe, Prince of. *See* Adolf

Schleswig-Holstein, Princesses of. *See* Helena, Princess Christian; Helena Victoria
See also Augusta Viktoria, Empress Consort of Wilhelm II, of Germany

SCOTLAND, King of. *See* James I (of England)

Sergeĭ Aleksandrovĭch, Grand Duke of Russia, 166

Singh, Sir Jagatjit. *See* Kapurthala

Sophia, Princess (of Great Britain), 74

SPAIN. (Sovereigns chronologically) *See* Fernando VII, Isabel II, Alfonso XII, Maria Cristina, Queen Consort of Alfonso XII, Alfonso XIII; Infanta of: Luisa (Princess Carlos of Bourbon-Sicily)
See also Katharine of Aragon (under Henry VIII); Maria de la Paz, Princess Ludwig Ferdinand of Bavaria

Sussex, Duke of. *See* Augustus Frederick

SWEDEN, King of. *See* Oscar II
See also Mariia (Princess William of Sweden), Grand Duchess of Russia

Teck (Since 1917 Cambridge), Prince of. *See* Francis; Princess of: Mary Adelaide
See also Alice, Countess of Athlone; Mary, Queen Consort of George V

Torby, Sofiia Nikolaevna, Grafinia, 161

U O Ĭ, 158

Umberto, Prince of Piedmont, 142

V M. *See* Mary, Queen Consort of George V

V R. *See* Victoria, Queen

V R I. Royal Library, Windsor Castle. *See* Windsor Castle

Vendôme, Duchess of. *See* Henriette

—Duke of. *See* Philippe Emmanuel

Victoire, Princess of France, 108

Victoria, Queen, 12, 84
See also Windsor Castle

Victoria, Empress Consort of Friedrich III, German Emperor, 85, VI

Victoria, Princess (of Great Britain), 42, 57

Victoria, Marchioness of Milford Haven. *See* Milford Haven

Victoria (unidentified label), 99

Villafranca, Comte de. *See* Charles Louis de Bourbon, Duke of Parma

W F. *See* William Frederick

www.ingramcontent.com/pod-product-compliance
Lightning Source LLC
Chambersburg PA
CBHW072144170526
45158CB00004BA/1500

9 7 8 0 9 4 4 2 8 5 8 2 4